IN HIS

TIME

Ms Baxter

*Ben
Onwuelezi
469-226-6132*

BEN-EL ONWUELEZI

Ben Onwuelezi

In His Time: Remembering Dad

NewVent Enterprises, LLC books may be ordered through booksellers or by contacting:
NewVent Enterprises, LLC
P O BOX 1253
Rowlett, TX 75088
Website: www.newvente.com
Email: info@newvente.com

Scriptures and references taken from the Clarke's Commentary, Kevin Griggs, The Daily Bible Plan, KJV, NKJV, New International Version (©1984), New American Standard Bible (©1995)

Because of the dynamic nature of the Internet, any web addresses or links contained in this book may have changed since publication and may no longer be valid. The views expressed in this work are solely those of the author and do not necessarily reflect the views of the publisher, and the publisher hereby disclaims any responsibility for them.

Publisher's Note: This book is a work of fiction. Names, characters, and incidents are products of author's imagination and revelation. All characters are fictional and any similarity to people, living, or dead, is purely coincidental. However, the revelation or vision and dreams integrated and depicted in this book are not fictional. They are real, foretelling of future events which are beginning to unfold before our very eyes.

ISBN: 978-0-9898733-0-7
Library of Congress Control Number (LCCN):2013949857
D-U-N-S number: 07-910-1251
Printed in the United States of America

TABLE OF CONTENTS

PREFACE

I wrote this book because things are not always as they appear. In other words, I believe events in our world are not as random as one would think but rather they are precipitated by spiritual activities. You often hear the expression tossed around in conversation, "nothing seems to make sense anymore". However, from a biblical point-of-view, our present-time events were perfectly foretold by Jesus Christ. Matthew 24:12 (NASB) states, *"Because lawlessness is increased, most people's love [of God] will grow cold."* Consequently, the end result becomes complete apostasy; people falling away from their faith and standing apart from the truth.

What is the meaning of these things? Biblical scholars differ greatly as they tell you it is the beginning, or it is the middle, or it is nearing the end of the "End Times" as described in the Bible. I am only a pharmacist by profession and not a biblical scholar, so I ask for forgiveness in advance, if any of my writings fall out of context or are not presented well. But I do know what Joel 2:28 tells us will happen in the last days: an outpouring of God's Spirit will lead to prophesy, dreams and visions. This is intended to warn us, yet also strengthen the faith of believers. Events in Syria, Iran and the Middle East at large, may lend credence to End Time prophesies.

Such revelations are certainly worth looking into. The following is one such revelation received on September 8, 1957 in Modesto, California by late Rev. J.S. McMullen. It is depicted in his book, *70 Years of Living Experiences, I Walked with Him.* I was a student of his at Cornerstone Assembly of God Church in Rowlett, Texas. This is an excerpt of that vision. You can read the rest of it, as well as others, embedded in the dreams of one of the characters in this book.

"...The cloud was moving southward to Syria and as it arrived at the border of Syria, there was a great explosion and out of the explosion came an army of men, of tanks, planes and weapons of war. To the west in the Great

Sea, were many ships, battleships. The air space over Israel and the adjoining countries were immediately taken up with planes of various nations. The land of Israel was like a beehive. It was swarming with soldiers.

The land and the air space resembled a Fourth of July fireworks stand on fire. The roaring of the planes, the impact of the big guns, the fire and the smoke from the devastation of war, the great clouds of smoke and the flashes from the discharges of mammoth guns. The Middle East became a slaughter pen.

During the battle, I heard someone say, 'Look over there!' I looked toward the land of Israel and there was a gun pointed toward the East and it discharged, it resemble a type of fireworks because it had a multiplicity of sparks, something like the glistening glitter of stars in the planets of heaven, similar to a show of fireworks on a Fourth of July evening..."

Modern Day Shepherds

I also wrote this book to highlight some challenges that ministers of the Gospel of Jesus Christ face. They are not super humans devoid of emotions. They are responsible as teachers and shepherds for the spiritual welfare of their congregations. They are answerable to God for such responsibilities and their leadership. But what happens if there is not adequate affirmation of support, financially or otherwise from the congregations?

Even now, some of our pastors are barely getting the necessary support to keep their ministries going. The majority of people in any given congregation do not meet their obligations with respect to giving offerings and tithes. The tithe is a 10% obligation, not an optional choice to decide whether one gives 1%, 3%, or whatever. Some have the mind set that this is the pastors' church and given 10% would be used for personal things. First of all, it is the church of Jesus Christ and not the pastors'. If you suspect lack of financial accountability in your local church, approach the pastor and his board for explanation instead of premature and unsubstantiated assumptions. But by not meeting our obligations, the church struggles to pay the pastors and staff members among other things. Now the pastors are not just concerned about our spiritual well-being but also worry about making ends meet in their own families. Some pick up secular jobs to augment their church salary.

The story of Moses and the children of Israel in transition from Egypt to the Promised Land is a classic example. Despite all the things the Lord did for them through Moses' leadership, they were still group of unappreciative men and women. Consequently, only two people (Joshua and Caleb) from the original exodus of individuals made it to the Promised Land. Even Moses himself, though he saw the land, never entered into it.

It is not unusual today, to find depressed and even suicidal pastors in the churches around America. Even Elijah and Moses suffered through these thoughts at one point or another in their ministries. They begin to question their callings, whether they have made mistakes by going into ministry. What can we do as a body of Christ to combat issues like this?

Churches at the Crossroad

This book also seeks to address the moral dilemmas our pastors and churches are facing in this age of political correctness and moral relativity. We claim our society is on a moral decline, yet we cannot voice the Truth. When we do, we are ambiguous about it. The passivity of the church, coupled with several judicial rulings, has become a contributory factor to the moral decay of American society. Though it may appear to be social progress and the advancement of American society, one cannot help but ask: what is it costing us?

Prayer and the Bible are objected to in schools but condoms are readily available in dispensing machines in many communities. In the past, you had to be at least seventeen years old to buy the "morning after" pill without a prescription, now courts have removed that age requirement, making it possible for girls of any age to buy such pills.

Sodom and Gomorrah were wicked and abominable cities and as

such they were destroyed. There were not even ten God fearing people in those lands, as that would have stayed the hands of the destroying angels. I pray that there are still enough God fearing people in America, as to convince God from judging us at this time.

In America as well as Europe, the governments have sanctioned the killings of their future generations, the unborn. Our politicians appear wise in their own eyes, yet are spiritually blind and lacking true wisdom. Does it make sense that if someone kills a pregnant woman, he would be charged for two murders, yet snuffing the life out of the unborn, as Dr. Kermit Gosnell did in Philadelphia in the name of "pro-choice", is tolerable? Why are we then, sarcastically speaking of course, so enraged over the deaths of those school children in Connecticut who were cut down by bullets yet we couldn't care less for the unborn that are violently terminated as well with knives? How can any modern society step on and trample down God's precepts and commandments and not expect to suffer the consequences?

Mathew 2:18 – A Biblical Analogy

"A voice is heard in Ramah, weeping and great mourning, Rachel weeping for her children and refusing to be comforted, because they are no more." - Matthew 2:18 (NIV)

In the highly regarded, *Commentary of the Bible* by Adam Clarke (emphasis added), we find the following:

"In Rama was there a voice heard - These words, quoted from Jeremiah 31:15 were originally spoken concerning the captivity of the ten tribes; but are here elegantly applied to the murder of the innocents at Bethlehem [insert Newtown, Connecticut or the United States at large]. As if he had said, Bethlehem at this time resembled Rama; for as Rachel might be said to weep over her children, which were slaughtered or gone into captivity; so in Bethlehem, the mothers lamented bitterly their children, because they were slain."

"...This mourning may refer to cases far from uncommon in the east,

where all the children have been massacred. The lamentations of a Hindoo mother for her child are loud and piercing; and it is almost impossible to conceive of a scene more truly heart-rending than that of a whole town of such mothers wailing over their massacred children."

Currently, the United States does not have enough young people to support our labor force or our retirees. Abortion has become the birth-control-method-of-choice in all fifty states. Homosexuals do not reproduce and heterosexuals of reproductive age care more for their careers than having large families and often don't have more than one child.

In the United States, our know-it-all politicians think the solution can be found with immigration, both legal and illegal. We are already home to almost twelve million illegal aliens and we continue to resort to the exploitation of underdeveloped nations and their educated class by enticing them with a "visa lottery" and an impression of a better life in the West. More and more, these immigrants are coming from nations with opposing religious and cultural beliefs.

It is just a matter of time before the weeds choke-off and outgrow the seeds. These new comers are gradually and systematically tearing and breaking down our way of life, culture, and religion and with the help of the court system in the name of separation of church and the state or in the name of assimilation. The United States would not have these problems had we not aborted so many babies who would have lived and in turn reproduced thereby preserving our way of life and beliefs.

A Biblical Line-in-the-Sand

The church of Jesus Christ, irrespective of the denomination, needs to speak with one voice. Our churches and members ought to draw a Biblical line-in-the-sand that says to the political leaders, "If you cross certain Biblical thresholds, that you are on your own and you should not expect the body of Christ to support or vote for you, period." Unfortunately this is easier said than done as the politicians continue to find ways to make the body of believers compromise their beliefs with futile promises and the false impression that they really "feel their pain". Is the church so gullible that she falls for that rhetoric each and every time?

In California, Proposition 8 was a proposed amendment to the state constitution to that "only marriage between a man and a woman is valid or recognized in California. The proposition passed the 2008 state elections with a majority of more than 52%. Yet in 2013, five members of the Supreme Court of the United States dismissed the will of millions of people. Five against millions!

Politicians believe that the majority of voters are ignorant and stupid, that we have no right to determine what is acceptable or not in our own communities. Perhaps, the politicians are right if we constantly cast our votes for people who foolishly make us believe they "feel our pain". We must decide what is most important to us and then vote accordingly and intelligently.

I realize that some people will not agree with some of the things I have written. My words are not intended to cause harm or provoke outbursts of unjustifiable emotions. Rather, I hope to cause you to think deeper, and examine your actions or inactions from a Biblical perspective.

Ben-el Onwuelezi

ACKNOWLEDGMENTS

This book would not have been possible without the support and encouragement of my beautiful wife and five lovely daughters. Thank you for understanding my long nights at the computer.

I would like to thank my editor, Richard, and all the folks at Exodus Design for their invaluable suggestions to improve the readability of this book.

Personally, I want to acknowledge God for His presence and for giving me the ability to complete this project. After many sleepless nights of writing and revising, I thank God for making this book a reality. I hope you will enjoy it and I ask that you recommend it to friends and families. To Him be the glory!

CHAPTER 1

WORRIES AND CONCERNS OF PASTOR SANTANA

Pastor Benjamin Santana was always very worried in his spirit that the two things he had been praying about for some time now may not come to fruition before he passes on. He kept his concerns and worries to himself except, perhaps, his wife, Marcella. These were issues he talked to God about, issues he believed only God could accomplish. He is almost 70 years of age and in poor health. His eyes are getting dim from the complication of diabetes and his blood pressure is not faring much better. It bothers him at times that he has to take so many medications to control his many health issues.

He has prayed and has read the word of God and His promises within. He knows and firmly believes in what the Prophet Isaiah wrote declaring, *"...with His stripes we are healed."* (Isaiah 53:5b KJV) He agrees with Apostle John when he said, *"Beloved, I pray that you may prosper in all things and be in good health, just as your soul prospers."* (3 John 1:2 NKJV) It is eating him up that these passages have not come through for him. He has not seen the manifestations of Apostle John's proclamation. Nevertheless, he takes courage in knowing that His grace is sufficient for him now and in time to come.

Nobody except his wife really knows what is going on in his life. Most of his parishioners think that because he is a man of God, he is immune from the trials and tribulations of this world. Oh how lonely he gets sometimes. He listens, advises, counsels, visits, and prays for his members, but it seems the members do not reciprocate. Perhaps, it has not occurred to them that their pastor would welcome their visitations to see how things are going on in his life.

Wouldn't it be nice if they could take him and his wife to dinner once in a while, go bowling or to see the Texas Rangers, the Mavericks, or the Dallas Cowboys play? It seems the only people he talks to are fellow ministers and they are often times be talking about the challenges they are facing; such as not attracting enough people to the church, dwindling church members, or not having sufficient financial resources to meet their church programs. They all take solace in the fact however, that it is He and not them that would build His church. Nevertheless, the pastor continues to fight a battle of doubt in his spirit as to the materialization of the needs that weigh his body, spirit and soul down. On occasions of this battle, he is always reminded by God promises and assurances:

"Look unto Jesus, the author and finisher of our faith."

"Cast all care upon Him, for He cares for you."

"God, you are not a man that you should lie…"

"'I know the thought that I think toward you', says the Lord…"

CHAPTER 2
LILLY OF THE VALLEY CHURCH

"In your time, O God", he always prays. Pastor Santana has been pastor at the Lilly of the Valley Church in Dallas, Texas for the past 15 years. It is a non-denominational church that has its roots with handful of migrant workers from Mexico, South and Latin America. The Church is situated just south of the central railroad, where the poorer immigrants reside. North of the railroad is where you have the middle to upper-class residents. It was because of the influx of new residents to the south of the railroad; that Pastor Santana would lead a handful of these people in setting up the small church.

They did so for various reasons as opposed to attending a church just North of the railroad or any other church for that matter. Some of the reasons were cultural differences, language problems, and the liberty to worship the best way they knew how. They were poor simple men and women and they didn't think they fit in well with the residents north of the railroad.

Jesus Morales said, "There are probably going to be people out there that won't like us, though they are going to smile at you and pretend like they do, but their smile doesn't mean 'you are welcomed', but rather can be interpreted to mean 'what are you doing here'"?

Cristofer, a black migrant worker who identifies himself as Bight of Biafra Ibo from Hispaniola-an amalgamation of what was once French speaking Haiti and Spanish speaking Dominican Republic-told of what he observed when he was going to a local church in West Texas. Members of this church were of different races and cultures from just about anywhere that you can think of. This church unfortunately had its ups, downs, innuendos, and faulty assumptions. And so it remained until the percentage of a certain group of people in the church began to rise and that correlated with the drop in the number of another race. He even overheard a couple talking about moving on to another church down the road for fear that their daughter is getting too close to boys of a particular race.

Ariel recalled an incident that happened to him several years ago that kept him away from a church for a very long time. He recalled that when he came to this church, the main service was about to begin, the man at the door, the usher, looked at him and asked if he was looking for the black church down the road? He stood and contemplated, but how would he know if he was looking for a black church or not? In his funny broken English, he stammered, "No! No! Me came to look for...to worship!" Sensing the uneasiness in the usher's face and his own feeling of apprehension, he turned away and left before he could finish what he had wanted to say.

These kinds of stories were what prompted Pastor Santana, Jesus, Cristofer, Ariel and few others to try and establish a church where they would be at liberty to worship however way they see fit. They believed that wherever the Spirit of God is, there is liberty. And at the Lilly of the Valley Church, they hope and pray that the spirit of God would come and dwell in it all the time.

CHAPTER 3

NEIGHBORHOOD OUTREACH MINISTRY

The neighborhoods on both sides of the track were growing; Pastor Santana's church, Lilly of the Valley is growing too. The church's outreach program and the old fashioned evangelism under the leadership of Pedro Santiago from Dominican Republic had resulted in many new members. Often times you would find him and his friends among migrant workers as they congregate and be waiting to be hired for work. He encourages them with his own life stories.

He would tell them, paraphrasing 1 Corinthians 11:23, "I want to give to you that which I also received. Seeing some of you here standing or sitting in anticipation for work brings back memories. You want to work, to make money to look after yourselves and your family but jobs are hard to come by. You probably don't have documentation to work, no friends; no one cares it seems. Even when you find work, you always be looking over your shoulder for immigration. Let me tell you my brothers, some one cared for me and he also cares for you. He name is Jesus Christ. We were all alienated from God, the Father until Christ came and made us legal before Him."

He would often offer them water and tamales, which they eagerly

5

consumed. He would tell them, "These things are good for your bodies, and we need them to live. But in an hour or so you will be thirsty and hungry again. I want to tell you that if you believe in the Lord Jesus, you will never be spiritually hungry and thirsty." He reads to them John 6:35 where Jesus Christ states, "I am the bread of life. He who comes to me shall never hunger, and he who believes in me shall never thirst..." He explained to them that their spirit needs to be fed with the Word of God more than their bodies need to be fed with tamales.

Occasionally, he would stuff some envelopes with money and give them away to men with families. Those men, on their way home from yet another uneventful day, would at least buy their children bread and milk. He believed he was doing what God wanted him to do.

Pedro and his friend's ministry to undocumented workers always hoped to accomplish one thing; to introduce them to the gospel of Jesus Christ. They realized that some of them eventually would be deported back to the country where they came from. If they could reach them with the gospel, then they would take it back to their homeland should they be deported. They believed this is one of the ways Matthew 28:19 would be fulfilled, making disciples of all the nations. They likened their mission in a positive way to sort of an ant mound and poison laden food sprinkled around the mound. As the ants take the bait deep into the colony, the colony is destroyed. Positive in the sense that their message is not a message of death and destruction, but rather a message of salvation, of life in Jesus Christ, of reconciling us to His heavenly father by His birth, His life and ultimately His death.

CHAPTER 4

EXPANSION AND CHALLENGES OF A GROWING CHURCH

Because of the rapid growth of Lilly of the Valley Church, Pastor Santana was going to have to move the church elsewhere or try to buy a vacant lot next door to build a bigger church. He was in dire need for a children's church, preteen and teenager's meeting rooms, a bigger nursery, a bigger sanctuary for adults, and more Sunday School classrooms.

The pastor met with his church Board of Directors to discus their options. First, the deacons and deaconess' decided to pray and fast daily for seven days. For each of the first six days, they would fast and pray for one hour, and then go around the perimeter of the vacant lot. On the seventh day, they fasted and prayed for seven hours, then walked around the lot seven times. This was their wall of Jericho. As they walked, they prayed according Deuteronomy 11:24, "'Every place on which the sole of your feet treads shall be yours.' Now let it be done according to your word for our feet have touched this land and we claim it."

The Board granted their approval for the purchase of the land and at the appointed time, they approached the seller. Not only did they buy the one acre they had prayed for, they bought the remaining four acres at an unbelievably low price. The pastor, the Board, and the congregation

7

were very happy and of course, they gave thanks to God who made it all possible.

All involved quickly learned that acquiring the land is one thing, but building is another. The issue became how to raise money, lots of money for an architectural design and construction. An architectural drawing of the proposed new structures, though it costs a lot of money, is only the first step. Getting it approved by the local municipality is much more difficult. The land was for zoned commercial because of its proximity to the railroad except when a special use permit is given. The church found itself pitted against a few well connected local businessmen from the area. They argued that if given the permit, the church would become a hub for illegal aliens thereby impacting the surrounding businesses negatively.

The church argued that their mission in the expanded facilities would not be any different from what they are already doing at that location; which is to seek the lost and to turn their faces to the cross of Christ, and to seek out for those who hunger and thirsty for righteous. They reminded the City Council of how and why the Lilly of the Valley Church was started, the drawbacks that would come to the community if permit was denied.

The church learned that some members of the Council were being used as a "wedge" by another party that had been interested in purchasing the land. Shortly before the owner of the land sold it to the church, he had discovered the plans that the other group had for the land. He didn't want his property to be used for a new "gentleman's club". He didn't see anything gentle about the intended use of the land. Therefore, he sold his land to what he called "a soul saving and not a soul destroying business". After much discussion and prayer, as well as a few "veiled threats" by others in the community to expose certain Council Members' alliances with the group that was opposed to the church, the city backed down. The battle was won, the walls of Jericho fell.

Pastor Santana was able to secure a loan from a local bank by using as the five acres of land that the church owned as collateral. He was very grateful even though the amount of the loan was significantly less than what he had been asking for. They didn't have anything else of value to offer as collateral to secure additional funds from the bank.

They decided to proceed at once with their ambitious project using the funds they had secured from the bank. They all agreed that waiting to secure all of the funds needed for the church building might take a very long time. They began taking pledges, especially those of them who had jobs. Others contributed labor or whatever they could. There were more people who pledged labor than money. They also planned to go back to the bank after a while for more loans. They were determined to see this project through.

CHAPTER 5
A JOURNEY OF FAITH

When the construction of the Lilly of the Valley Church began, it started with much hope and enthusiasm. As the economy continued to decline, money was much harder to come by, making the purchase of building materials very difficult. Those who had made pledges were having a very difficult time redeeming them as many were no longer working and several had been forced to move to other cities or states for a variety of different reasons.

The loss of Sergio really hit them hard. He had left for Costa Rica at the advice of his attorney for immigration reasons. He had gotten himself involved in a marriage relationship and he needed to leave United States for a short time after which he would be back. Not long after he left, his wife filed for divorce and moved in with his best friend. Sergio was stuck and the attempts that were made to bring him back proved unsuccessful. He lost thousands of dollars for the marriage contract, all of his personal belongings, a truck, and his work tools to his ex-wife. He became another victim of a "marriage of convenience", a process that has become very profitable for some.

The slow pace of the work began to weigh heavily on Pastor Santana's spirit. He would always pray for God to bless his members financially. He told God how most, if not all his members had given everything they had for the construction of the church building. At the same time, he would tell his members the story of the widow's mite, her faithfulness and subsequent blessings. On occasions, he felt very guilty for referencing that Scripture in order to encourage the members to do more. He was quite aware of the trials and struggles of his congregation. They had pledged in good faith, believing that God would make a way for them.

Interestingly enough, the neighborhoods on both sides of the track continued to grow. The church north of the track has broken ground for a huge cathedral. At least that's what the architectural drawing on a sign board depicting the size and shape of the completed building says. Some of pastor Santana's members were able to find work here, laying bricks, carpentry, or whatever. So whatever money they made here was reinvested in their own church building project and that kept the work going.

Pastor Santana loved his congregation and joyfully watched as a few members actually received the blessings of God. However, they did not honor Him with their tithes and offerings and have also chosen not to redeem their pledges. These individuals think they have "arrived", because of their new status in society and they began to look down on their comrades. Pastor Santana remembers quite well their humble beginnings, how he comforted them with the word of God. He always reminded them to first seek the kingdom of God and His righteousness, especially in this culture with so many trappings and distractions, and He will meet their hearts' desires. He told them that it is God's desire that they be in good health and to prosper, but they must be obedient to his Word and all of his commandments. He told them God makes way where there is no way, even in foreign lands.

He would remind them of the story about Joseph, Gods plan for him, and his faithfulness which brought that plan for his life to fruition. Unfortunately, some have fallen through the cracks and became victims of riches illusion. They seem to be wavering, one step forward and two steps back. They are hardly seen in church and when they come, they are there for self-promotion and to "show off". Is it almost like saying, "Look at me now, I have made it and I did it all by myself, my own way!" They must have been listening to Frank Sinatra.

This is the impression one got looking at Antonio. Antonio was once a very dedicated member. But ever since he started his tire business, things have changed a lot; his mannerism, his attendance to church and his involvement in the things of the Lord. Instead of coming to church on Sundays, he chose to be open for business. Pastor Santana always reminded Antonio and others like him, not to forget their first love and their prior commitment to the Lordship of their Savior, Jesus Christ. He would often quote Matthew 22:21 saying, *"...So give back to Cesar what is Cesar's and to God what is God's."* Finally, he reminded them that their ultimate goal is their heavenly father's business in this world. He retold the story of Joseph and Mary searching Jerusalem for three days, only to find the young Jesus in the temple and Jesus asked them, "Why did you seek me? Did you not know that I must be about my Father's business?" (Luke 2:49)

CHAPTER 6

PASTOR SANTANA'S RETREAT

As the months turned to summer, Pastor Santana would retreat to the mountains to meditate and to pray for about two weeks. This year, his heart was more sorrowful and he couldn't wait to get up there and pour out his heart to his God. Whenever he is downcast, he draws strength from Philippians 4:6-7, "*Be anxious for nothing, but in everything by prayer and supplication, with thanksgiving, let your requests be made known to God, and the peace of God, which surpasses all understanding, will guard your hearts and minds through Christ Jesus.*" Then he remembered Hannah as an example of someone whose supplication or humble petition to God did not go unanswered.

Usually, before he makes this annual trip to the mountain retreat, he turns the pulpit over to his young assistant, Pastor Ricardo Nunez. Pastor Ricardo is about the same age as Pastor Santana's son. This time he told Pastor Ricky, as he is popularly known, that there is a possibility he might stay up there a little longer to wait upon the Lord.

On Sunday afternoon, after the morning service, he departed to the mountain side, but not before charging them to be prayerful. Some of the members were worried about him, they could see the anguish on his face and they understood some of the reasons. Nevertheless, they promised to be in an attitude of prayer and they bid him farewell.

Meanwhile, the big cathedral north of the railroad was almost completed. What a majestic, beautiful building it has become. "If the people who are going to be worshipping here would worship as beautifully as this building is, the spirit of God would come down each time He is called upon", commented Fabian, one of the workers. "But God doesn't dwell in man-made temples, regardless of how majestic they looks; He dwells in us." interjected a coworker. They all nodded in agreement.

CHAPTER 7

TRIALS AND STRUGGLES

As often was the case, Antonio and his friends would gather under a big oak tree for discussions and to share stories in Spanish, most of the time during their lunch breaks. They talked about everything and anything, about their families, how hard it is making ends meet with the money they make. Some of their problems stem from the fact that they were undocumented workers who are in the country illegally. Securing meaningful employment was almost impossible except when one would resort to illegal schemes such as using somebody's social security card or number to work or engaging in a false marriage relationship.

To make things worse, the down-turn in economy was really squeezing them hard. Most employers are not hiring and the few that did, were constantly being watched to make sure illegal workers are not hired. Fidel believes that the cat and mouse game between them and the United States Immigration Officers, keep them on their toes and in constant worry and fear of being deported if they are caught. Also, the newly enacted law in the state of Arizona had them worried. They were concerned that other states might begin to enact similar legislation. On top of that, many of these people were leaving Arizona and moving into their neighborhoods and that doesn't make things any easier for them. "Just two weeks ago," Fidel said, "Immigration Officers raided the meat-packing plant where some friends were working, and most were taken to detention, pending deportation hearings."

Nevertheless, they were all very thankful to God that in spite of their circumstances for they had managed to support their local church, the Lilly of the Valley, their families here in the United States as well as those remaining in their native countries. They talked about the cathedral they are helping build and the difficult times they are having building theirs. They discussed Pastor Santana's son, Manuel who had turned his back from the teachings of Christ because they believed Satan has hardened his heart and marked him for destruction. They thought out loud if there was anything they could do to lighten their pastor's burden as far as finishing up with their church building or with whatever else they perceived he needs them to do; after all the Bible talks about bearing one another's burden.

At this junction, Antonio's younger brother, Julio, suggested that they all pray and commit pastor Santana, wherever he is at the moment, into God's hand. He reminded them how their pastor asked them to always remain in an attitude of prayer. He also reminded them of the Scripture in Matthew 26:36-46. Jesus Christ and His disciples were in Gethsemane. They were all very tired from their travels. Jesus asked Peter and two others to stay awake and keep watch while He prayed. When he had finished, he saw that his friends had fallen to sleep. An hour of prayer was all He had requested of them but they could not even do that.

Antonio and his friends believed that Christ won the battle for our redemption in the garden at Gethsemane and not on the tree at Calvary. The shedding of blood and His death on the cross only sealed the victory at the garden and to fulfill biblical prophecies. They believed it was an intense spiritual battle, with the devil continually poking at Him, "Are you sure you want to do this?"

The devil showed Him the road to Calvary and the sufferings that would be asked of him, "Do you really want to do this?"

The devil must have perceived weakness, for the Bible recorded He was exceedingly sorrowful, deeply distressed and falling on his face he prayed, *"My Father, if it is possible, may this cup be taken from me..."* Then the devil came back and poked at Him again, "Are you sure you are up to this?" Christ walks away from the devil to check with Peter and the others, but He finds them sleeping.

He must have been surprised that they were sleeping, considering the raging battle currently going on, for He said to them, *"What! Could you not watch with me one hour?"* At this point, Christ was indeed alone!

He came back to his vantage point, in agony and distress. His sweat became blood as He prayed in response to devil's poking. *"O my Father, if this cup cannot pass away from me unless I drink it, Your will be done."*

Antonio and his friends believed these sequences of events and interactions with the devil happened three times as were His temptations in the wilderness after forty days of prayer and fasting. There were valuable lesson to be learned about the Gethsemane experience. Antonio and his friends did not want to be asleep or in slumber as their pastor is facing such difficult challenges, they must stand in the gap and pray as they promised they would do. Before they started to pray, they meditated on the song "Sweet Hour of Prayer"

Sweet hour of prayer! Sweet hour of prayer!

That calls me from a world of care,

And bids me at my Father's throne

Make all my wants and wishes known.

In seasons of distress and grief,

My soul has often found relief,

And oft escaped the tempter's snare,

By thy return, sweet hour of prayer!

Sweet hour of prayer! Sweet hour of prayer!

The joys I feel, the bliss I share,

Of those whose anxious spirits burn

With strong desires for thy return!

With such I hasten to the place

Where God my Savior shows His face,

And gladly take my station there,

And wait for thee, sweet hour of prayer

As they bowed down their heads, Jesse was prompted to start praying. He began in Spanish: "Dear God in heaven, who is everywhere, who has all power to do anything, we thank you in Jesus Christ's name for such an opportunity as this. We want to lift Pastor Santana up to you wherever he is at this very moment. His spirit is heavy laden, we can feel it. We now cast his care upon you, father God, for you care for him, we pray for your peace which surpasses all understanding to be with him. We know that there is nothing he desires more than to have Lilly of the Valley of the church completed. We lack the means to accomplish the work before us and we know that nothing short of miracle can accomplish this task. We thank you for this beautiful cathedral we are helping build and we hope that one day we would worship you in a completed Lilly of the Valley Church.

"Also, we commit pastor Santana's son, Manuel into your hand. He doesn't know you and he is lost in sin. Please, father, cause his heart to seek your face, make him turn away from his sinful ways to you. We love pastor Santana very much and we would like you to meet his heart's desires. Give us energy and strength to do our work, protect us from falls, injuries and other accidents. Bless us spiritually and financially; bless our families in Jesus Christ's name we have prayed, Amen."

Jesse's prayer was so powerful as to move some of his friends to tears. Though for one of the men in this group, the reason for the tears had nothing to do with the words he had uttered in the prayer. Rather, he was a new convert and just a few months ago, he was not very receptive to the Word of God and he looked at his friends with disdain. He must have known what his friends where thinking, for he loudly declared, "What the Lord did for me, he will do for Manuel".

"Hurry up with your lunch for it is almost time to return to work", David urged them. Reuben reminded them that the sooner they finish their work for the day, the more time there would be for their soccer practice.

CHAPTER 8
MR. KEVIN CHRISTIANSON

Jesse's prayer was heard by more than just his group of co-workers gathered under that tree for their lunch break. Unbeknownst to the work crew, there was another individual resting nearby. He had his head down on the bench like somebody sleeping. Kevin Christianson was a middle-aged white man, yet he understood Antonio and his friends quite well even though they were speaking Spanish. He used to live in Paraguay where he had a successful building supply company coupled with a contracting business. He came back to the United States three years ago due to health issues; he needed to be close to his health care providers. Poor health notwithstanding, he had managed to open and run a successful building supply company since coming back to America. It was through a former associate that he landed this job as a sub-contractor for the cathedral.

Work neared completion at the cathedral. It has taken just one year and no expenses were spared. It is a beautiful-looking state of art church building. The main church is big enough to accommodate almost five thousand people at one given time. It is then surrounded by complimentary buildings such as the children's church, nursery, youth center, library / bookstore. Antonio and his friends could not be any happier for members of this church. Their only wish was that God would swing the door wide open for them to enable them to finish their own church. They tried to fight off the spirit of resentment or jealousy and they constantly reminded themselves that good things are just ahead of them. Because they did such a marvelous job building the cathedral, they are hoping that the contractors and members of the church would be in need of their services in the future for work. They were indeed exemplary workers and very well liked by everyone.

The next Sunday didn't look or feel any different than the previous ones. As usual, the Sunday School classes were partitioned with moveable screens and are conducted in the main church building because of a lack of available spaces. It is not unusual to hear what is been taught in another class even though the teachers make a conscious effort to keep their voices low. Sunday School lasts one and a half hours followed by the main service.

The main service began with an opening prayer, followed by the recognition of visitors, followed by their welcoming song:

And I love you with the love of the Lord

And I love you with the love of the Lord

I can see in you the glory of the Lord

And I love you with the love of the Lord.

Then the superintendent summarized the Sunday School lesson for the benefit of those who were not in attendance. Next were the announcements by the assistant pastor, an update on pastor Santana's retreat, an update on the progress of the new church building, an update on money pledged and money redeemed, as well as another passionate plea for more contributions.

When the pastor asked if anyone had a testimony or praise report, Antonio stood up on behalf of his friends and testified how much they have been blessed from their work at the cathedral and how it had helped bring him and his friends closer in the things of the Lord. He said that he senses in his spirit that God is about to open the windows of heaven and shower His blessings on them and the congregation at large. As show of faith, he and his friends would pledge a majority of the money they had earned that month working on the new cathedral. Many of the women pledged to provide food for the workers in the coming days ahead.

Interestingly, three visitors to the church for the first time were not noticed during the service. They were associates of Kevin Christianson, sent in to survey the needs of the church. Their extensive experience in the construction supply business allowed them to make quick assessments of the needs of this church without asking any questions or drawing any attention to themselves. They wrote their pledges for the necessary building supplies and placed the envelope in the collection plate during the time of offering and thanksgiving. They quietly slipped out of the building shortly after.

Now it was time to hear the Word of God as Pastor Ricky was handed the microphone. As it is customary with the church before sermons, he started to sing:

I have a wonderful treasure,

The gift of God without measure

I would travel together, My Bible and I

As they get to "My Bible and I', everyone would raise their Bibles up high. Some young people raise their Smart Phones and iPods, as those were their primary sources of reading the Bible. Pastor Ricky continued:

The old, old story is forever new,

The old, old story, praise the Lord 'tis true

That Jesus died for me as well as you,

I love the old, old story.

The title of the sermon delivered by Pastor Ricky was "A Measure Given, A Measure Received—to whom much is given, much is also required". "What are in your hands, what has God placed in your hands, how much of it are you willing to give to Him?" he asked the congregation. "He gave us His best, Jesus Christ, what can you give Him"? He quoted Matthew 8:10 that says, *"Freely you have received, freely give."* Here is what we have freely received and what is expected of us citing Kevin Griggs in The Daily Bible Plan:

"Freely we have received His grace and mercy, and freely we should extend that grace and mercy to others. Freely we have received His forgiveness of our sins, and freely we should forgive others of their transgressions. Freely we have received His encouragement, and freely we should encourage others. Freely we have received His wisdom, and freely we should share that wisdom with others.

Freely we have received His love, and freely we should show that love to others. Perhaps the most important thing we have received from God is the Good News about Jesus Christ. Each of us has been saved by His grace through faith in Jesus, and the fact is that at some point in our lives we learned about our Savior because someone somewhere cared enough about us to share with us the Gospel. God freely gives us salvation, but in order for people to receive His gift they have to first hear the Good News, and that is where we come in. Freely we have received salvation through His Good News, and freely we should share that Good News with others".

He delivered a very powerful message that touched every one deeply. At end of his presentation was a benediction and the service came to an end.

CHAPTER 9

SURPRISE!

Shortly after the building cleared out, the treasurer began to count the money that was collected during the service. It was then that he saw the pledge for the building materials that had been inserted into an offering envelope. He was taken aback for a moment, not knowing what to make of the pledge as there was no indication of who it was from. Was this for real or just a prank, he asked himself? He brought it to the attention of the assistant pastor and the church board to see what they thought. They were all completely puzzled as well. They decided to pray over it and to commit all of the pledges they had received to God so that He may bring the pledges to fruition.

For several days, nothing happened. No phone calls, no emails, no correspondence from the visitors who had pledged the much needed building materials for their church building. Doubts started creeping into the hearts of some, as to the authenticity of the pledge. Others prayed like they had never prayed before because they believed that their prayers were about to be answered.

Shortly thereafter, a huge contingent of people descended on the church premises. They came with all types of building materials, equipment and tools. They came with measuring tapes and surveying devices to measure and re-measure the buildings under construction for additions and improvements. They had been able to get copies of the building plans from the local government, and they knew precisely how and where to make improvements and other changes as long as the contractors and the church board would allow them to do so.

The church's architectural board and the assistant pastors were quickly summoned to the building sites; they were presented with an updated architectural drawing of the church plans. They all loved it and they didn't have any doubt that pastor Santana would love it too. As a result, they gave their approval to make necessary changes to the original plan and the new plans were promptly approved by the local authority.

With all the bustling energy at the building sites, news of good things happening at the building site spread like wild fire. On Saturday of this particular week, Antonio and his friends had to postpone their scheduled soccer match until further notice in order that they may devote more time to what matters most to them, their church building. Their joy knew no bound and occasionally they would break out singing spontaneously:

Great is your faithfulness, O God my father

There is no shadow, of turning with you

All I have needed your hands have provided

Great is that faithfulness Lord God to me.

It was just a matter of weeks before pastor Santana would return from his retreat. "The church will be transformed!" said Jesse.

"Pastor Santana will be surprised" Miguel added.

"I think he will be more grateful than surprised." replied Antonio. "He is a man of faith, remember; he always talks about "In His time", God's time, how God has never failed him. I think this will only reinforce his faith in God."

More and more people were volunteering their time and services wherever they were needed at the church. It had become an avenue to witness to non-believers with the Gospel of Jesus Christ.

CHAPTER 10

A LOST SON

One afternoon, Saul began talking to a young man working next to him about the God of Abraham, Isaac, Jacob, and Pastor Santana. God can provide a way where otherwise there is none. He can help anyone mend his ways as long as that is their desire. The young man told him that he was a preacher's son and that he grew up in a church. He talked about how he started hanging out with the wrong crowd and how he started drinking hard liquor before graduating to using hard drugs.

To feed his addiction, he and his mischievous gang resorted to the illegal manufacturing of methamphetamine using pseudo ephedrine contained in products such as Sudafed. Cases like this prompted the state government to institute measures whereby one must present an acceptable identification and is limited to a certain amount of pseudo ephedrine that he or she can purchase at a given time.

The young man said that he almost died on two occasions from over dose, but that did not deter him from this illegal scheme. He was once been busted and sent off to jail for doctor shopping and trafficking in unauthorized prescription medications.

He said he remembers vividly his father telling him that "bad company will corrupt good manners" and how he advised him not to walk with the ungodly, nor stand with the sinners, nor sit at the seat of the scornful and instead, to know God, the creator of the universe. He thought that his father didn't know what he was talking about. But now, he believes his father was right and he thinks he has failed both his earthly as well as his heavenly father.

Saul drew closer to him and put his right hand on his shoulder. He told him that he is quite sure that both fathers love and care for him. He told him the story of the prodigal son and that of Jesus Christ, how out of love the prodigal son was received back by his father and out of love God sent his only son, Jesus Christ to die on the cross for our sins.

He told him how he had been saved and some of the things he was delivered from. He also told him that Jesus Christ came for people just like the two of them and that there is room for all at the foot of the cross and that Jesus is earnestly and tenderly calling. He told him not to let the gentle Savior pass him by.

He asked him if he would like to ask Jesus Christ into his heart so that he may experience the feeling of the Father's love once more. "Yes", the young man replied reluctantly.

Saul began to pray: "Dear heavenly father, I thank you in Jesus Christ's name for an opportunity such as this. My friend here is tired and heavy laden with the things of this world, please remove this load that is weighing him down and give him rest and peace that only you can give. He desires to have a relationship with you as well as his earthly father. Please bring him back to you that he may know a peace that surpasses all understanding. Draw him closer to you and turn his heart and eyes upon you and to focus on your wonderful face. I pray that you cause those things that weigh him down to become shadows in the light of your face. I pray that you Lord would do for this young man, what You did for me nine months ago. Forgive and wash his sins away in Your blood. I thank you again, Father, for what you have done for my friend here in Jesus Christ's' name we pray, Amen."

Quickly thereafter the young man left, even before Saul could ask him his name and to invite him to church. He didn't even get a good look at him either because he had worn a baseball cap in such a way to conceal much of this face. "Well," Saul he said, "I don't know his name but I am sure God knows his name and who he is."

CHAPTER 11
THE REVELATIONS OF PASTOR BENJAMIN SANTANA

As he lay down sleeping on his last night on the mountain, pastor Santana had two dreams which were very perplexing to him. He has had many dreams that have come to pass. He didn't know why these revelations are not plain, direct, and understandable. It is always like "the Sun, Moon, and the Stars bowing down to Joseph" or "seven ugly cows out of the Nile eating seven sleek and fat cows" or "seven thin heads of grain swallowing up seven heads of grain that were healthy and good."

He hopes once he gets back to his station that he would gather knowledgeable Biblical scholars to analysis and perhaps interpret those dreams. Nevertheless, he takes comfort from First Corinthians Chapter 13: 9-11 that says *"For we know in part and we prophesy in part, but when completeness comes, what is in part disappears"* (NIV). Here are his dreams or revelations:

First Revelation

Pastor Santana was swimming in a huge body of water. Next he found himself and his brother, Samson, perched on a platform high above the water. From this vantage point, they looked directly down on the body of water and watched the continents float freely on the water. They could also see some of the things going on in the world.

They wanted to get down back to the water, they didn't know how. They contemplated jumping down from the platform, but the distance was too great. They decided they had to climb down from where they were. As soon as Samson started to move, a brick or stone dislodged and they were forced to stop. This was not a safe path at all.

While still on the platform, they noticed a couple of people, possible three, came to this water with a fishing rod to fish. Eventually they got down to the water though he had no idea how it happened.

While Pastor Santana was in this water, he was standing upright and could still see all the continents scattered around. The water level and the continents were up to or just below his waist level. He had in his right hand what appears to be a long stick or staff and with that he started to move the continents to the left and to the right until they lined up in a straight line.

Second Revelation

From Pastor Santana's vantage point, high up in the stratosphere, he appeared to be flooding the earth with water by turning on a gigantic, out of this world, fire hydrant. He likened it to water pouring into New Orleans, Louisiana as the levies gave way when Hurricane Katrina came to visit. He saw water rise and rise to a great level. It was disaster of epic proportion to be likened also to the flood in Noah's time.

But then he saw one humongous building that seems to rise above the water. It had louver-type of windows at the very top and he got into the building through one of the windows. He also saw a few people came up from nowhere and got into the building through the windows as well. As he walked around inside this building, he did notice more people who made it in. He then took a position inside the building and lay down to sleep.

Then he woke up and became worried about these revelations, but he kept them to himself.

CHAPTER 12
THE RETURN OF PASTOR SANTANA

Three weeks later during Sunday morning's service, the church was filled to capacity. Many new visitors have been coming to the church for fellowship as they can identify with the church. Others have been coming as a result of witnessing efforts when they came to volunteer their services in the church building or from the "love your neighbor" neighborhood ministry. Overall, there were a great number of people who came in anticipation of Pastor Benjamin Santana's return from the mountains.

By this time, the atmosphere at the church had become quite extraordinary. Right from the time one walked in, the presence of God could be felt. You had a feeling that God was going to come down to consume the burnt offering if there was one, as was in the days of Elijah. However there was a different kind of burnt offering, the praise and worship music. The song leader led them from one spirit uplifting song to another. The bulk of the songs were in Spanish, yet one who doesn't speak the language can understand what is being sung:

When I look into your holiness

When I gaze into your lovely face

When all things that surround me become shadow in the lights of you

I worship you, I worship you,

the reason I live is to worship you....

Great is thy faithful, O lord my father

There is no shadow of turning with thee

All I have needed your hands have provided

Great is your faithfulness, Lord God to me...

The worshippers were totally lost in the spirit, so to speak, faces turned to God and hands lifted up. Pastor Benjamin Santana came in quietly and sat in the back as the next song was being sung.

He is my peace who has broken down every wall

He is my peace; He is my peace

Cast all your care upon him for He careth for you

He is my peace; He is my peace...

Then,

God is moving, by His Spirit

Moving in all the earth

Signs and wonders when God is moving

Move oh Lord in me

Then suddenly, a woman sitting in a front pew on the right side of the sanctuary started speaking in a peculiar language as the rest of the congregation kept quiet with their heads bowed. Her words were very strange:

Abum Chineke nke mgbochie, adighim agbanwe

Otum di nnyahu, otua ka m di ta, otuahu ka m g'adi kwa echi

Umum genum nti

Oburu na unu achosiem ike, unu g'achotam, m ga egosikwa unu
onwem,

Unu g'amakwa na mu onwem bu Chineke unu.

Anuwokwam akwa nile unu n'ebe maka ihe nile n'esobu unu

Ahuwo kwam ntukwasi obi unu n'ebe m no.

Anam asi ugbua, udo diri unu, odiworo unu nma.

Ozo, asim odiworo unu nma.

Umum ndi ikom na inyom, nyenum obi unu

N'asopuru unu iwum nile.

Oburu na unu asopurum, m g'ebuli unu elu.

Otua ka Jehovah nke usu nile nke ndi-agha siri.

After she was done speaking, there was dead silence. Then Kristopher, the Ibo Hispaniolian, having studied the Ibo language by correspondence, nervously stood up before the congregation and began to interpret in Spanish what he just heard.

I am the ancient of days; I change not

As I was yesterday, so I am today, so will I be tomorrow

My children listen to me

If you seek me, you will find me, I will show myself to you and you
shall

know that I am your God

I have heard all your cries about the things that worry you

I have also seen how you have committed your faith onto me

I said to you now, peace be unto you, it is well with you

I said again, it is well with you

My sons and my daughters give me your hearts

Obey my commandments

If you honor me, I will lift you up higher

Thus says the Lord of Host

The people were moved by the visitation of the Holy Spirit. An altar call was called for people to come forward to give their lives or to rededicate their lives to Christ. Scores of people came to the front as the song leader started singing:

Softly and tenderly Jesus is calling, calling for you and for me;

Patiently Jesus is waiting and watching, watching for you and for me

Come home! Come home!

Ye who are weary come home!

Earnestly, tenderly Jesus is calling

Calling, O sinner, come home

Oh for the wonderful love He has promised

Promised for you and for me

Though we have sinned, He has mercy and pardon

Pardon for you and for me.

At the end of the last stanza, a young man came forward that looked very weary and a bit disheveled. Only a very few recognized who he was. Of course he was known by his heavenly father, God; as well as his earthly father, Pastor Santana. Saul also recognized him as the young man that he had prayed for a few weeks back.

Pastor Santana walked up to the altar to help minister to the people giving their lives to Jesus. He looked a little thin but he could sense and feel the anointing of God upon him. He first approached the young man, who had his head down, and was standing in stooped posture. Pastor Santana gently touched the man's chin to make him look at him. The recognition was immediate as his eyes opened wide and tears began streaming out.

As the sobbing continued; he was then wrapped in the warm embrace of his father and surrounded by people that he grew up with in the church. Pastor Santana spoke softly, "Son, Jesus loves you and I love you too. We have never stopped loving you son."

Shortly thereafter, Pastor Santana addressed the congregation by telling them how good the Lord had been to him, his wife, and the church family. He began to explain to the congregation the meaning of what they had just witnessed. He asked rhetorically, "Why would God choose to speak to his people in a language other than what we can speak and understand, what does it really mean?"

He continued, "To start off my friends, He is the God of all flesh and He created all languages. So, if He can cause a donkey to speak to Balaam, as the Bible tells us in Numbers 22: 1-35, then He can certainly cause a little old Hispanic lady to speak in the South Eastern Nigerian Ibo language. As for the meaning, it is called speaking in tongues, that is to say being able to speak in an unfamiliar, peculiar language while in the presence of God.

The Bible tells us in 1st Corinthians Chapter 14 that some people in the body of Christ have the gift of speaking in tongues and some have the gift of prophesy. It tells us that the church is edified by the interpretation of tongues, as we have all witnessed today.

Speaking in tongues is a fulfillment of Jesus Christ's promise that was made to his disciples and it applies to us today. He told the disciples that when He was no longer with us here on earth, that he would send a comforter in his place in the person of Holy Spirit. So speaking in tongues are a manifestation of being filled with the Holy Spirit."

He directed them to the book of Acts of the Apostles Chapter 2 starting from verse one, "When the Day of Pentecost had fully come...And they were all filled With the Holy Spirit and began to speak with other tongues...such as Egyptian, Arabic, Libyan, and Asian languages to name but few. The people of the land were equally amazed to hear their languages spoken by people who never spoke any other language before other the Galilean language. The Apostle Peter explained what they had witnessed and about three thousand of them believed and became Christians."

From that day forward, Pastor Benjamin Santana believed and trusted God to supply and meet all of his needs. His son's acceptance of Jesus Christ as his Lord and personal savior and the completed Lilly of the Valley church served as a reminder to all the members of the church that God really does answer prayers. On that memorable Sunday, with hearts filled with thanksgiving and praise, the congregation lifted their voices and sang praises unto the lord;

This is my story, this is my song

praising my savior all the day long

This is my story, this is my song,

praising my savior all the day long...

CHAPTER 13

INTERPRETATIONS OF PASTOR SANTANA'S REVELATIONS

Two weeks, after that wonderful service, Pastor Benjamin Santana gathered together some of his friends. He shared his revelations with the hope that they might help decipher the dreams. He reminded them of Joel 2:28 and Acts 2:17: "In the last days, God says, I will pour out my Spirit on everyone. Your sons and your daughters will prophesy, your young men will see visions, and your old men will dream dreams."

Having heard of the revelations, the friends decided to go home and pray about their possible meaning and to reconvene in two weeks.

When the five friends gathered again in Pastor Santana's office, they sat around a large, circular table to discuss the assignment given to them. With their Bibles, notes, and other materials on the table, they began their deliberations by first praying and asking God for wisdom and clarity of mind and thought

Theo Sunnyvale

Dr. Theo Sunnyvale, a seminary professor, began by saying, "From the beginning, God has spoken to people through diverse ways and means such as by visions and dreams. So, with ever increasing activities in the spiritual realm and manifestations in the physical realm, we are all witnesses of the ending (not end) result; instability on Earth precipitated by Apostasy. In these unpredictable days, prophetic chattering, visions, and dreams shall also increase. They are warning signals that say, he who has ears let him hear and they say also, prepare the way for the lord and make straight paths for him. Therefore, we, the church ought to be encouraged, strengthened, and comforted.

"Unlike earthquakes", he continued, "that strike without warning, God's judgment is not without warning. His warning is this, **Fear God and give glory to Him, for the hour of His Judgment has come.**"

Andrew Sutherland

"As I ponder on these dreams, especially, the first one", said Andrew Southerland, Dean of local Bible Institute, "I can't help but think of God's judgment as well." He directed them to the book of Revelation 17:15, "Then the angel said to me, 'The waters you saw, where the prostitute sits, are peoples, multitudes, nations and languages'. Here are my thoughts on this revelation", he continued, "Water represents people of the world. Realignment of continents could be realignment of people in countries of the world as in the "Arab Spring" in the Middle East or as in Ezekiel chapter 38:2-6 or Revelation 17:12-14, against the people of God."

Ezekiel 38:2-6

"Now the word of the Lord came to me, saying, 'Son of man, set your face against Gog, of the land of Magog, the prince of Rosh, Meshech, and Tubal, and prophesy against him, and say, Thus says the Lord God: Behold, I am against you, O Gog, the prince of Rosh, Meshech, and Tubal. I will turn you around, put hooks into your jaws, and lead you out, with all your army, horses, and horsemen, all splendidly clothed, a great company with bucklers and shields, all of them handling swords. Persia, Ethiopia, and Libya are with them, all of them with shield and helmet; Gomer and all its troops; the house of Togarmah from the far north and all its troops—many people are with you."

Revelation 17:12-14

"The ten horns which you saw are ten kings who have received no kingdom as yet, but they receive authority for one hour as kings with the beast. These are of one mind and they will give their power and authority to the beast. These will make war with the Lamb, and the Lamb will overcome them, for He is Lord of lords and King of kings; and those who are with Him are called, chosen, and faithful."

Andrew Southerland continued, "As far for the man with a stick realigning the continents, the question becomes, who is he and what does he represents? Is he the prostitute, the beast, or the system of government that sits on many waters, that is over the peoples and nations? Again I am drawn to Revelation chapter 17, this time verses 7-11.

Revelation 17:7-11

"But the angel said to me, 'Why did you marvel? I will tell you the mystery of the woman and of the beast that carries her, which has the seven heads and the ten horns. The beast that you saw was, and is not, and will ascend out of the bottomless pit and go to perdition. And those who dwell on the earth will marvel, whose names are not written in the Book of Life from the foundation of the world, when they see the beast that was, and is not, and yet is. Here is the mind which has wisdom: The seven heads are seven mountains on which the woman sits. There are also seven kings. Five have fallen, one is, and the other has not yet come. And when he comes, he must continue a short time. The beast that was, and is not, is himself also the eighth, and is of the seven, and is going to perdition."

"That same chapter also talks about ten kings in alliance with the beast", Andrew Southerland added.

Revelation 17:13-18

They would be of one mind and they would relinquish their power and authority to the Beast until the word of God is fulfilled. For God has put it into their hearts, to fulfill His purpose, to be one mind, These will make war with the Lamb, and the Lamb will overcome them, for He is Lord of lords and King of kings; and those who are with Him are called, chosen, and faithful. And the woman whom you saw is that great city which reigns over the kings of the earth."

Dr. Ralph Mansfield

Dr. Ralph Mansfield of Dallas Bible Prophecy Institute began to explain some possible explanations for the staff and fishermen. "What might be the meaning of the staff by which he did the realignment?" he began. "Could the staff be a kind of ideology or authoritative apparatus used as a means of control by the prostitute or Beast? Could the staff stand for the judgment of God upon the earth? The staff in Moses' hand was used to bring judgment upon Pharaoh's house and the Egyptians. The staff represented the word of God, the power of God." He refers them to verses in Ezekiel 38 and 39 that state that those nations that have lined up against God's people would face God's judgment as Egypt did when she refused to let God's people go.

Ezekiel 38:16-23 & 39:1-8

"This is what the Sovereign Lord says: You are the one I spoke of in former days by my servants the prophets of Israel. At that time they prophesied for years that I would bring you against them. This is what will happen in that day: When Gog attacks the land of Israel, my hot anger will be aroused, declares the Sovereign Lord. In my zeal and fiery wrath I declare that at that time there shall be a great earthquake in the land of Israel. The fish in the sea, the birds in the sky, the beasts of the field, every creature that moves along the ground, and all the people on the face of the earth will tremble at my presence. The mountains will be overturned, the cliffs will crumble and every wall will fall to the ground. I will summon a sword against Gog on all my mountains, declares the Sovereign Lord. Every man's sword will be against his brother. I will execute judgment on him with plague and bloodshed; I will pour down torrents of rain, hailstones and burning sulfur on him and on his troops and on the many nations with him. And so I will show my greatness and my holiness, and I will make myself known in the sight of many nations. Then they will know that I am the Lord."

"Son of man, prophesy against Gog and say: 'This is what the Sovereign Lord says: I am against you, Gog, chief prince of Meshek and Tubal. I will turn you around and drag you along. I will bring you from the far north and send you against the mountains of Israel. Then I will strike your bow from your left hand and make your arrows drop from your right hand. On the mountains of Israel you will fall, you and all your troops and the nations with you. I will give you as food to all kinds of carrion birds and to the wild animals. You will fall in the open field, for I have spoken, declares the Sovereign Lord. I will send fire on Magog and on those who live in safety in the coastlands, and they will know that I am the Lord.

"I will make known my holy name among my people Israel. I will no longer let my holy name be profaned, and the nations will know that I the Lord am the Holy One in Israel. It is coming! It will surely take place, declares the Sovereign Lord. This is the day I have spoken of."

"As for the meaning or significance of the presence of the fisherman on the body of this water, here is what I think," continued Dr. Mansfield. "If the body of water represented peoples, multitudes, nations and languages according to Revelation 17:15, then the fishermen are really fishers of men or people. The question then becomes, what kind of people were they fishing for or were they fishing randomly? Does this speaks of the rapture of the church or does this speak of the separation of the wheat from the chaff as the kingdom of heaven is at hand as described in Matthew 3:12?"

Revelation   **17:15**

"...The waters which you saw, where the harlot sits, are peoples, multitudes, nations, and tongues."

Matthew 3:12

"His winnowing fan is in His hand, and He will thoroughly clean out His threshing floor, and gather His wheat into the barn; but He will burn up the chaff with unquenchable fire."

Dr. Mansfield then stated that the dream also refers to Revelation 14:14-20:

Revelation 14: 14-20

"I looked, and there before me was a white cloud, and seated on the cloud was one like a son of man with a crown of gold on his head and a sharp sickle in his hand. Then another angel came out of the temple and called in a loud voice to him who was sitting on the cloud, "Take your sickle and reap, because the time to reap has come, for the harvest of the earth is ripe. So he who was seated on the cloud swung his sickle over the earth, and the earth was harvested. Another angel came out of the temple in heaven, and he too had a sharp sickle. Still another angel, who had charge of the fire, came from the altar and called in a loud voice to him who had the sharp sickle, "Take your sharp sickle and gather the clusters of grapes from the earth's vine, because its grapes are ripe" The angel swung his sickle on the earth, gathered its grapes and threw them into the great winepress of God's wrath. They were trampled in the winepress outside the city, and blood flowed out of the press, rising as high as the horses' bridles for a distance of 1,600 stadia."

He concluded his remarks by stating, "Let us not forget **The Proclamation of Three Angels** told in Revelation 14:6-13. One angel proclaimed with a loud voice, 'Fear God and give glory to Him, for the hour of His Judgment has come; and worship Him who made heaven and earth, the sea and springs of water'. Then the second angels declares that, 'Babylon is fallen, is fallen, that great city, because she has made all nations drink of the wine of the wrath of her fornication.' Finally, the third angel warns against worshipping the beast and his image, or receiving his mark, otherwise one drinks of the wine of the wrath of God."

Dr. Laurel Rockwall

Laurel Rockwall, an end time prophetic scholar, continued with the point that Dr. Mansfield had just made. "I believe that the first and second dreams are related and interwoven. She started by explaining what "waters rise up" meant. "It is a metaphor for the assembling of an army." she stated. "Waters is a common prophetic image for a multitude of people as we saw in the first dream. Waters rising up out of the north or a down pouring of water from the north, means an army of men, which should come in great numbers, and with great force and rapidity, like an overflowing flood against the people of God." She referred everyone to the following Scriptures: She clarifies her statement referencing passages in Jeremiah 47.2., Isaiah 8:7-8, Isaiah 17-12-13. Ezekiel 38: 1-6, 8-9 invading army coming like a storm, covering the land like a cloud), 15-16

Jeremiah 47:2

This is what the LORD says: "See how the waters are rising in the north; they will become an overflowing torrent. They will overflow the land and everything in it, the towns and those who live in them. The people will cry out; all who dwell in the land will wail."

Isaiah 8:7-8

"Therefore the Lord is about to bring against them the mighty floodwaters of the River, the king of Assyria with all his pomp. It will overflow all its channels, run over all its banks and sweep on into Judah, swirling over it, passing through it and **reaching up to the neck**. Its outspread wings will cover the breadth of your land, O Immanuel."

Isaiah 17:12-13

"Thus says Yahweh: Behold, waters rise up out of the north, and shall become an overflowing stream, and shall overflow the land and all that is therein, the city and those who dwell therein; and the men shall cry, and all the inhabitants of the land shall wail."

"Perhaps, these waters rising out of the north are an army of men that shall descend upon Jerusalem or God's people like a flood but will not conquer it as the "head" remains above the water. It reaches up to the neck only. The "head" above the waters means that the Lord Jesus Christ himself will crush these armies of men that have gathered together against Jerusalem or the people of God." she concluded.

Authors Commentary:

The dreams shown to Pastor Santana are not new. Similar dreams and visions have been reported by many others around the world in recent years. After fully comprehending the explanations of the characters written above, the question then becomes, how would these armies with their instruments of war be gathered against the people of God and not raise an alarm? Perhaps, the subsequent action or inaction of President Obama of the United States against Syria over the use of chemical weapon in their civil war might be a contributory factor. Now, you have Saudi Arabia, Egypt, etc. on one side of the Syrian war and Iran, Muslim brotherhood, Hezbollah on opposite side and also threatening to attack Israel. There will come a point in time perhaps, when these nations will flip like a light switch and join forces against their arch enemy, the state of Israel. Russia is already a player in the conflict; China may, perhaps, tag along.

This perhaps points to what was shown to Rev. J.S McMullen 1957 depicted in his book, *"70 Years of Living Experiences: I Walked with Him"*.

I looked to the land of Russia (Magog); I saw mountains, valleys, factories, horses, armies and plains. I saw soldiers by the thousands around her borders. Afterward, I turned to the south to Turkey, Syria, Transjordan, Jerusalem and Egypt as well as Iraq, Iran, Saudi Arabia, plus others. Israel looked so small among the other nations. I saw tanks and planes going into Syria. I saw train loads of equipment and implements of war going into Syria. When I saw this, I said, "That little nation could be pushed out into the Mediterranean Sea." I looked toward the sea and it was covered with ships, and on the ships in large embolden letters was U.S.A. As I turned back toward Russia, I saw a great flash and a great cloud causing the elements to turn to darkness.

The cloud was moving southward to Syria and as it arrived at the border of Syria, there was a great explosion and out of the explosion came an army of men, of tanks, planes and weapons of war. To the west in the Great Sea, were many ships, battleships. The air space over Israel and the adjoining countries were immediately taken up with planes of various nations. The land of Israel was like a beehive. It was swarming with soldiers.

The land and the air space resembled a Fourth of July fireworks stand on fire. The roaring of the planes, the impact of the big guns, the fire and the smoke from the devastation of war, the great clouds of smoke and the flashes from the discharges of mammoth guns. The Middle East became a slaughter pen".

During the battle, I heard someone say, "Look over there!" I looked toward the land of Israel and there was a gun pointed toward the East and it discharged, it resemble a type of fireworks because it had a multiplicity of sparks, something like the glistening glitter of stars in the planets of heaven, similar to a show of fireworks on a Fourth of July evening. Pieces of flaming matter fell into a company of Russian soldiers. It seemed to set off a chain reaction, jumping from man to man and men died by the thousands, yea millions. This perhaps is a new weapon which will be used in the last battles.

I saw many Russian soldiers gathered around the Persian Gulf and the Spirit of Prophecy said "These are Russia and her satellites." There were many ships in the Arabian Sea. The Spirit of Prophecy came forth saying, "These belong to the nations against Jerusalem." The planes began to fall, ships sank, bodies, one on another making great heaps and blood covered the ground. The Spirit said, "Battle of Nations."

As I looked from the Middle East to New York City, I saw ships scattered over the Atlantic Ocean. Then quickly, I canned the Pacific Ocean until I sighted San Francisco. In the streets of the two cities, hundreds of people were milling about. Out of the Pacific and the Atlantic Oceans, almost at the same time, simultaneously, there came a blast, which looked and sounded as though the oceans had erupted. As I looked upon these great cities of our nation, I saw the skyscrapers of New York and the buildings of San Francisco begin to sway and crumple to the ground. Where I had seen thousands of people in the streets, now there were only a scattered few.

I heard a voice and it sounded as it came over a loud speaker. The voice said, "America, try to have courage. It seems that God has forsaken us". Many Christians came to me and asked, "Brother McMullen, what are we going to do?" The Spirit of God moved heavily upon me and within me and through prophecy I said, "The Lord will provide".

After I had spoken these words, I looked toward the East and saw something which looked like two stars or two headlamps of an automobile shining through fog. They appeared brighter, and as it came closer, the cloud vanished and I saw that it was the Lord Jesus Christ. He looked so large and so beautiful. He stood in mid-air and as a great magnet; people were drawn to Him from all over the world. The heavens were filled with people from the nations of the world. In a few minutes, they were gone.

Again, I looked over Palestine and the Middle East and it was covered with dead bodies, with horses, with wrecked planes, tanks with demobilized implements of war. I said, "Lord, you said that Russia would be defeated on the hills of Palestine." The Spirit said to me, "Look, look". I looked to the north and saw an army, but it was a very small army and they were marching very slowly. Their clothes were dirty and torn. The spirit said, "She was defeated. Behold, only a sixth part of her."

As I witnessed all of this, I said, "Oh my Lord, Thy Judgment are sure."

The Lord appeared and came near to me. I have never seen anything as loving and as kind. Here is what He said to me, "Remember, Jesus was once offered for the sins of many and unto them that look for Him shall He appear the second time without sin unto salvation." (Hebrew 9:28)

We know that we are living in the closing days of time. Jesus said, "And when these things begin to come to pass, then look up and lift up your heads, for your redemption draweth nigh." (Luke 21:25-28)

Rev. J.S. McMullen
Sept.8, 1957
Modesto California
From his book: *"Seventy Years of Living Experiences: I Walked with Him"*

55

Should President Obama fail to punish Syria for crossing the line he drew in the sand—paying a price for the use of chemical weapons or weapons of mass destruction—one cannot help but wonder what message it portrays.

Inaction will signify to the state of Israel that the current leaders in Europe and America cannot be trusted to deal with nuclear issue in Iran. They exhume the appearance of toughness, but they are really timid and indecisive. It will be obvious sooner or later that the security of Israel would not come from United States of America or European nations but from He who neither sleeps nor slumbers.

Perhaps, the state of Israel alone would have to travel 2000 miles to Iran to dismantle their nuclear facilities. Having come to a full realization that trusting present day Obama's administration or perhaps future Hilary Clinton or Joe Biden's administration or security council of the United Nations will be detrimental to her very existence, Israel will not have too many options left but to unleash unprecedented attack on Iran and her allies. This action will definitely unleash retaliatory attacks from Hezbollah in Lebanon and Iran of course. Other parties would eventually join in the conflict. The Middle East indeed would be literally on fire and some part of it might even be swallowed up the Mediterranean Sea.

CHAPTER 14

SOON COMING MESSIAH CHURCH (SCMC)

While the Lilly of Valley Church was rejoicing for God's goodness, the big cathedral north of the railroad, now known as SCMC, is dealing with very different types of issues. Many of its members seem to think the kingdom of God is a real estate property up for sale. Either they never read or they had forgotten the story of the rich young ruler. They thought that if they give large sums of money for the work of God instead of their hearts, that they are in good standing with the Lord. Some seemed to forget that the Bible says, it is not of works, lest one boasts and it is neither by one's power nor might. Some of the issues facing this church were capable of causing divisions in the church if not handled properly.

With the completion of SCMC, the senior pastor retired, as he had said he would do. Under his leadership for almost twenty years, the church grew in number and became financially stable. This is a church that was struggling in some areas which the outgoing pastor had difficulties tackling. One of the reasons was the long term relationships he built up with some principal figures, which put him at a disadvantage to effectively deal with the issues in the church.

These were the issues that the fifty year old new pastor, Tim

Summertime, would have to deal with as he had no alliances in the church yet. One of the issues was the known infidelity among those in position of authority. Pastor Summertime intended to deal with this issue very discretely at first, by asking the offenders to stop such practices and to repent. But if they failed to heed his admonitions and that of the church board, he would have no choice but to suspend them and to relieve them of their duties. The last measure was to kick them out of the church and there would be no compromises.

This was a difficult task, but it had to be done to purify the church of Christ. One of the consequences of such a position however could involve an attempt by the powerful people in the church to make him resign. But didn't actually believe they could muster enough support to force his resignation, but if they tried and failed they would likely pull away and divide the church. Pastor Summertime doesn't think that this church or any church that claims to be a member of the body of Christ should be a place for social engineering or a place for political correctness. He was looking forward to a church where people would worship God in truth and spirit as opposed to people described in 2 Timothy 3:1-9, "...Lovers of pleasure rather than lovers of God, having a form of godliness but denying its power..."

He prayed that the Lord would give him the wisdom, good judgment and the temperament to handle problems such as these. He was frequently reminded of Apostle Paul's letter to Timothy, to preach the word, convince, rebuke, exhort, with all longsuffering and teaching.

Another issue that became a burden of the new pastor concerned the falling away from the faith by the young people, both in his congregation and the church of Christ at large. It bothered him that once these young people, who were raised up in the church, leave their homes and go off to college, many of them seem to forget who they are in Christ. Instead of being Christ's ambassadors and unashamed of the gospel as stated in Romans Chapter 1:16, they allow themselves to be corrupted and swayed by peer pressure and new age philosophies.

He struggled with the question of what the church should be doing to reverse this trend. These young people are the future of the church and he knew something was not right when their faith and belief were compromised so easily. He firmly believed that the church would not be able to fully understand the depth of the problem until they could identify the reason it was happening.

It saddened him that the congregations in most churches today were comprised of middle-age or elderly people. At times he would take his members to task by asking, "Do you know where your children and grandchildren are at this very moment?" He would frequently preach from 1Peter 2:21, "For you have been called for this purpose, since Christ also suffered for you, leaving you an example for you to follow in His steps". He would ask, "Whose steps are they following: yours, Christ's, or the world's? Did you do enough teaching, praying, and admonishing to hold their feet to the fire of the Holy Spirit when they were living under your roofs?"

CHAPTER 15

FALSE TEACHINGS AND INDOCTRINATIONS

Pastor Summertime acknowledged the fact that there were professors, sororities, and other interest groups in institutions of higher learning that were seeking to destroy these young minds by false indoctrination and by subtle teaching of things contrary to the word of God. He heard from some in his congregation that references to some Eastern Religion (ER) beliefs were been fed to young and inexperienced minds.

He likened what was happening to the **Parable of the Sower** in Matthew 13:1-9. "...some (seeds) fell on stony places, where they did not have much earth; they immediately sprang up because they had no depth of earth. But when the sun was up they were scorched, and because they had no root they withered away. And some fell on thorns, and the thorns sprang up and choked them".

He believed that the use of non-biblical jargon were the thorns that are choking the shallow-rooted, spiritual life of our young people in institutions of higher learning. Some of the subtle teachings that were being used to deceive these young minds included:

False Teaching: "We must work with him (Christ), rejoice with him, serve with him, and behold him in every object and in every person we meet".

Reality: "It is finished" were the last words Christ uttered on the cross. He did it all; His work was done. He alone paid the price for your sins and mine. It wasn't a joint venture. We rejoice in Him! We are not going to serve with Him; the Bible tells us that we would reign with Him. Christ is not coming back as a servant but as King of kings and Lord of lords. The Bible doesn't say that you can behold Him in every object and in every person. Rather, He (His Spirit) dwells in us once we accept and acknowledge Him as our redeemer and savior. He neither dwells in a man-made object nor unrepentant souls.

False Teaching: "We should love all our dear ones, and enjoy their comradeship by seeing Him (Christ) in them. We should stride always to realize that they are manifestations of God. We are spirit; they are spirit. Spirit loves Spirit".

Reality: Not according to the Bible! Can an evil spirit, for instance, love the spirit of God or Christ? If the answer is no, then the spirit doesn't love spirit in this regard. If the same Spirit that quickens Christ from the dead is not in you, then you have the spirit of the antichrist. Christ came to destroy the works of the devil and not pat him on the back for those works.

False Teaching: "To progress spiritually we must dwell constantly with the thoughts of Christ".

Reality: Having the mind of Christ is the way to spiritual growth. Philippians 2:5 says, "Let this mind be in you which was also in Christ Jesus." Interestingly, non-Christians think of Christ constantly, but the question becomes, do they have His mind?

False Teaching: "You can not expect to attain Christ's Consciousness unless you live perpetually in Him."

Reality: How do you attain the consciousness of God the Son? The Bible says John 1:1-4, "In the beginning was the word (Christ), and the word was with God (Father) and the word (Christ) was God. He was in the beginning with God. All things were made through Him (Christ), and without Him nothing was made that were made. In Him (Christ) was life, and the life was the light of men". When you are in Christ, you are a new creature because old habits must have passed away. We strive to be like him (Jesus Christ) and not to be God like He is.

These types of unbiblical teachings and thoughts convinced Pastor Summertime that we were losing many young minds to the darkness. He knew he must address this issue in his next sermon.

He told his members that they must be very careful where they are sending their children to for higher education. "Make certain they are well grounded in the biblical teachings" he preached. "Just because a child is eighteen or nineteen years old, doesn't mean they are emotionally, psychologically, intellectually and spiritually matured to be thrown into the lion dens of liberal universities."

Then he turned and faced the young people to address them. "My heart is saddened by the plight of our youths and our college bound young men and women. I always made mention of you in my prayers so that our God would help you to be an over-comer wherever you may find yourself. There will be challenges, temptations and trials to test your faith. Your so called friends will entice you to go check out that topless joint or to go have a drink or to indulge in premarital sex for fun. I tell you the truth, they don't have your best interest at heart, stay away from friends like that. I remind you once more of Apostle Paul's admonition to young Timothy to flee youthful lusts.

"Now turn to Proverb Chapter 31 and read; 'Give not thy strength unto women, nor thy ways to that which destroyeth kings. It is not for kings, O Lemuel; it is not for kings to drink wine; nor for princes strong drink: Lest they drink, and forget the law, and pervert the judgment of any of the afflicted. Give strong drink unto him that is ready to perish, and wine unto those that is of heavy hearts.'

"If and when your friends want to make you think that sex is cool and everybody is engaging in it, remember it is a lie from the pits of hell.

I want you to remember the story of Elijah. He thought he was the only one of the Lord's prophets whereas Baal has four hundred and fifty prophets. Afraid and fearful for his life he fled to Mount Horeb. He was asked twice by God what he was doing on the mountain. God commanded him to 'Go back the way he came.'

"Contrary to his belief that he was one of the only prophet of God left, God told him that He has reserved seven thousand in Israel. All of whose knees have not bowed down to Baal and whose mouths have not kissed him. And I say to you likewise there are thousands if not millions of young men and women like yourselves that have not bowed down at the altar of immorality and who have not yielded themselves to unrighteous behavior.

"You must know that, you will not find solace and comfort in booze, wild parties and sex but rather disappointments, depression, diseases, destruction, and death. The wages of sin are death. I urge you to listen to the quite voice of the Holy Spirit saying to you, 'What are you doing here' should you find yourself where your faith is about to be compromised.

"You must know that your bodies are temples of the Holy Spirit, who is in you, whom you have received from God. You are not your own; you were bought at a price. Therefore honor God with your bodies.

CHAPTER 16

A TRAGIC TALE

The pastor's message that Sunday would be in the form of a story. A tragic story! This was a story that gripped the attention of not only the youth, but everyone in the church that morning. Sadly, it came at the expense of one of Pastor Summertime's best friends while he was growing up. It was the story of Caleb Fisherman.

Caleb was born in the church and accepted Jesus Christ as his Lord and Savior earlier in life, when he was about twelve years of age. By the time he turned eighteen, many of his peers were going off to college, but he chose to go on a medical mission with his girlfriend, who later became his wife. They had two lovely children by the time he was twenty four. Having traveled to quite a few countries in South America, they decided to come home because they were home sick and their parents wanted to see the grandchildren. He decided he needed to go to college to further his education.

At twenty five years of age, he enrolled in a liberal college for Religious Studies. He wanted to study about the beliefs of other religions such as Islam, Hinduism, Buddhism, New Age movements as well as cult practices. He wanted to study the differences and similarities if there are any between these religions and Christianity. He chose to attend a liberal college because it was microcosms of the society at large. He felt he could be an ambassador and a witness for Christ there as well.

One of the many pieces of advice he was given, was to guard his faith as described in 1Corinthians 10:12-14. "If you think you are standing strong, be careful, for you, too, may fall into the same sin. But remember that the temptations that come into your life are no different from what others experience. And God is faithful. He will keep the temptation from becoming so strong that you can't stand up against it. When you are tempted, he will show you a way out so that you will not give in to it. So, my dear friends flee from the worship of idols"

Those advising him knew that there had been many incidents where one sets out to investigate the merits of an association or group and ended up being sucked-in into that association or group. This was to be Caleb's fate.

He studied very hard, but he wanted to be a practical student too. He felt he needed to attend every meeting, Christian or non-Christian to which he was invited, as well others to which he was not invited.

The road he was traveling was very sloppy and slippery, the sooner he turned back, the better it would be for him. But, when a friend invited him to attend a midnight party by the "CD" Club, he gladly accepted his invitation out of curiosity.

It was a pool-side event and it started with small talk, socializing and drinking. Some were swimming and others were engaged in other activities such as reading palms as a game. At the nudging of his friend who told him it is a benign and fun game, he had his palm read, though reluctantly. The young woman proceeded to tell him, "Dude your hands are clean!"

"Of course they are, I wash them regularly like most people do" he replied.

"You know, many of these people here have Obsessive Compulsive Disorder (OCD) in hand-washing, yet their hands are not as clean as yours. Hmmm, are sure you belong here?" she asked.

"You see, I told you it is fun", says his friend laughing.

Whether he was thinking of what the young woman told him in a physical realm or not, one cannot tell. But the fact remains that demons know who is who and they often times would make utterances to your true nature through their chosen or inhabited vessels. A case in point was seen in Acts 19:16, "But the evil spirit said to them in reply, Jesus I know, and Paul I know; but who are you?"

He was being told that he did not belong at this gathering but he did not heed the warnings. Later on, new members and guests were welcomed and toasted with a drink offering to "CD" with some rapping incantations.

Many of the new members didn't know what they are getting into. As far as they know, they are having a good time at this midnight pool-side party. They did not know that "CD" stood for Children of the Devil, a cult movement whose motto is a twisted commandment of Jesus Christ, "Love one another as I have loved you"

They believed that since Christ was partly God and human, that attaining the divine and spiritual love of Christ is not possible. Since He knows we are merely mortal beings, substituting His love for a carnal one would probably be fine with him.

They drank blood in fulfillment of Christ's commandment, when he said, "Drink, this is my blood which is shed for many for the remission of sin." They interpret the Bible out of context to attract naïve young Christian men and women who think this is another campus ministry.

They believe their master comes out after midnight, following the drinking of blood mixed with Kool-Aid and other additives and after many incantations as rap music. To please their master, they would engage in what seems like ordinary flirtations in the eyes of any regular observer and culminating into giving themselves over to the demonic goddess of love and carnality.

Caleb continued to attend to "CD" midnight parties every Saturday, Wednesday, and Friday. He thought that he could win these people over to Christ by his associations to them. He wanted to be like Paul who said in 1Corinthians 9:11, "To the weak I became weak, that I might win the weak. I have become all things to all people that by all means I might save some."

The members of "CD" are not stupid; many of their practices were kept away from him until the right time, in order to peel off his faith gradually. They knew who he was and they were deliberate in their attempts to win him and others like him over to their side.

They chose their meeting days and times carefully. Saturday was chosen in order to prevent, as they called them, "church goers" from attending church on Sundays. They figured out that if they can have them all night long on Saturday, entertain and show them good time, that they would be weak physically and spiritually to attend to church on Sunday or midweek services on a Wednesday.

Caleb failed to test the spirits to know if they were of God or maybe he knew the spirits were not of God, but he wanted to stick around to lead them to the cross. He was about to learn a lesson that he would never forget as long as he lived.

CHAPTER 17

THE SAMPSON THEORY

The "Sampson Theory" is based on finding the source of someone's strength and power, then disabling it gently and deliberately.

The closer Caleb got to "CD", the farther away he got from the God he loved. The hunter was becoming the hunted.

Just as the spirit of God left King Saul, the spirit of God left Caleb. He became troubled by an evil spirit. Things had fallen apart spiritually and physically and he had no one to turn to for help. He was like a drowning man, grasping and struggling to stay afloat. He was almost melancholic, schizophrenic, and in a state of madness. He was in no position to continue with his education. He started exhibiting aberrant behaviors, seemed to have extra power, seemed like he is wired from lack of sleep even with increasing amounts of sleeping tablets beyond normal recommended doses. Even anti-psychotic medications did not seem to work.

While at the hospital, additional laboratory tests and a CT scan were ordered by the attending physician. He was hoping to find something in those tests that might help show the etiology of this affliction. There was no tumor or any abnormal neurological findings detected in his brain. He tested negative for hallucinogens, amphetamines, cocaine, narcotics and opioids.

Because of the escalation of young people who are buying up pseudo ephedrine containing products and converting them to amphetamines by crude method, his blood was tested and it came back negative as well. However, a sample of his stomach content showed a thick, tarry, blood-like substrate. He was examined by a gastroenterologist for possible bleeding into the stomach and the result was negative. A pathologist was brought in to analyze the content of the thick fluid extracted from his stomach.

His condition became a point of discussion with a medical group on rounds with the attending physician. The team was comprised of medical students, clinical pharmacists, and one nurse who was also a nutritionist. The issue raised by the attending physician was, given the findings or the lack there of, and given that there was no history of mental instability that they knew of, how should they begin to deal with this young man's situation?

One medical student, Craig, suggested giving him a common anxiety medication to calm him down, followed by stronger anti-psychotic medications if necessary. Another medical student suggested doing some investigative work, to reach out to families, friends, and associates. He believed that might shed some light as to his back ground, his whereabouts, or any events prior to this episode.

But Craig insisted that Caleb be given the anti-anxiety medication now and they could wait for other tests and back ground checks. The attending physician agreed and ordered an anti-anxiety medication to be given intravenously, and then the team moved on to check on the progress of another patient suffering from opioid withdrawal.

Interestingly, the nurse knew something about this young man that the rest of the team didn't know. She knew Caleb's parents from her church. She had attended the church for several years until she relocated because of her job. She knew this boy when he was growing up in the church; she was there when he accepted Christ as his Lord and personal savior and his subsequent baptism. She knew his was a life consecrated by the blood of Christ.

When she entered his room to inject him with anti-anxiety medication, she hesitated. She remembers seeing a case like this before since she started working at this hospital. She went and stood to the right side of the bed, then she put the palm of her right hand on his forehead as when a mother checks her baby's temperature, he seemed to calm a bit. Turning his face to the left, she noticed the letters "CD" tattooed on the back of his ear lobe. She knew what that letters stood for and what the young man was up and against.

She locked the door behind her and squirted the medication into the sink. Then she called Caleb's parents and his pastor to alert them of his situation. She wanted them to come to the hospital and take him home before the doctors damaged him even more with psychotic medications and their serious side effects.

First she found Revelation 12:1 on her Blackberry phone and read to Caleb, "And they overcame him because of the blood of the Lamb and because of the word of their testimony," She then scrolled to Ephesians 6:12 which states, "For we are not fighting against flesh-and-blood enemies, but against evil rulers and authorities of the unseen world, against mighty powers in this dark world, and against evil spirits in the heavenly places." This is indeed going to be a spiritual battle.

She urged him to say the words, "Jesus Christ is Lord" but he refused. She started repeating it herself over and over again. "Jesus Christ is Lord, Jesus Christ is Lord, Jesus Christ is Lord." Suddenly he curled up into the fetal position and started staring at her with the look of a mouse caught in a trap.

He looked afraid. She could have called this demon to come out of him at that moment, but she didn't. She didn't want the demon moving around the hospital, there were enough of them already causing havocs in the lives of many of the patients. Her intention was to reactivate the flow of Jesus' blood in him to make the demon very uncomfortable.

Indeed, this demon had not found a resting place in this young man ever since he started troubling him.

She remained with him until his parents and pastor arrived. They requested the young man be released to their care. At the sight of his parents, and pastor, Caleb became agitated and combative. His father raised his voice and commanded him to be quiet "in the name of Jesus." He instantly became quiet to the amazement of the attending physician and the team, except the nurse. Demons indeed know authority.

CHAPTER 18

BATTLE LINES DRAWN

Caleb was brought back to his parents' house. Waiting there were his wife and children, some of his closest buddies from the ministry and several prayer intercessors from the church.

An altar was set up in the living room reminiscence of the God's instruction to Moses in Numbers 21:8: "Make a snake and put it up on a pole; anyone who is bitten can look at it and live" or as in John 3:14, "Just as Moses lifted up the snake in the desert, so the Son of Man must be lifted up."

Once at the house, he became restless again, not agitated but mourning in girlish voice, "I'm so tired, please let me go. I haven't done anything to you."

"Who asked you to speak? I rebuke you in the name of Jesus Christ", responded the pastor. The demon was bound, but not yet cast out.

They directed the young man's attention to the altar with one crucifix, but he was reluctant to do so. His father raised his voice and asked him, "Does the cross mean anything to you son? Look up to the cross, I say look up to the cross and be saved!" Then they start to sing:

At the cross, at the cross

Where first I saw the light

And the burden of my heart rolls away

It was there by faith I received my sight

And now I am happy all the way

After almost an hour of praise and worship, his oldest daughter, about 6 years old, began demanding to see his daddy. They had said no to her initially, for they feared this demon would jump over to this weaker vessel, the child. Now they felt confident this would not happen.

She approached her father, stretched out on the floor, as the grownups stood all around him. She knelt beside him and turned his face towards her with the palms of her hands. She said to him, "Dad I love you, but Jesus Christ whom we serve loves you even more. Tonight you shall be well again." Then she gently turned his face back to the cross. "Dad, we are going to sing the songs you taught me to sing", she told him. "I am sure you remember these ones:"

In the name of Jesus

In the name of Jesus

We have the victory

In the name of Jesus

In the name of Jesus

Demons must have to flee

When we stand in the name of Jesus

Tell me who has the power to oppose

In the name of mighty Jesus

We have the victory

Then,

Jesus breaks every fetter,

Jesus breaks every fetter,

Jesus breaks every fetter,

And away it flew

Now let us sing hallelujah

Let us sing hallelujah

Let us sing hallelujah

Let us sing hallelujah

And away it flew

As the daughter went back into the other room, the group began to pray fervently with God's word. The pastor lifted his voice and spoke; "We are now going to exercise His power that is at work within us. Lord, your word says in Matthew 16:19, 'I will give you the keys of the kingdom of heaven; whatever you bind on earth will be bound in heaven, and whatever you loose on earth will be loosed in heaven.' The Lord told us in Mark 16:17, 'and these signs will accompany those who believe: In my name they will drive out demons...'"

They began speaking in heavenly languages. In these various tongues, they bound the demon, and ordered it to come out of the young man, in the name of Jesus Christ! Instantly, a girlish looking creature appeared and immediately bolted out the door, slamming it as she departed. The group began to sing:

There is power, power wonder working power in the Blood of the Lamb

There is power, power wonder working power in the precious Blood of the Lamb,

Amen.

The young man had been delivered. He looked tired, but he sat up and started praising the name of the Lord.

The next morning, the neighbor's dog was found dead in the nearby lake. He said the crazy dog all of a sudden took off running for no apparent reason.

Pastor Summertime had never told that story before. He wanted it to be a lesson for the youth in the church to be mindful of joining fellowships or associations whose activities may look benign at face value but when weighed against Biblical precepts, fall flat. He always worried that these young Christians were not knowledgeable enough in the Bible and they could easily be led astray by empty, feel good messages.

As he finished and closed the service, he looked around the sanctuary. Not a single person was stirring or making their way to the exits. Every head was bowed and he could hear scores of parents weeping for their sons and daughters. The youth sat in stunned silence as the impact of the story continued to wash over them like waves in the ocean. Pastor Summertime never expected this reaction to the story, but as he dropped to his knees, he whispered praises to the Lord above. No one in that church would ever forget that story.

As he stepped down from the platform, the church secretary quietly approached him and handed him a note. He had been asked to attend an emergency meeting of ministers in downtown Dallas to discuss the latest events in the Middle East. The Sovereign State of Israel was preparing to launch a massive attack on Iran. He dropped to his knees once more and prayed for wisdom...

To be continued…

A TRIBUTE TO DAD

CHRISTIAN AYOZIE ISRAEL ONWUELEZI—Chris or Ayo as his friends called him, was the middle son of Chief Israel Oparaiwu and Katherine Onwuelezi. He was born on September 20, 1926 in Mbieri, a suburb of Owerri, capital of the state that would become Imo in the country of Nigeria on the continent of Africa. It is said that he was born with silver spoon in his mouth, hence the name Ayozie (uwa). He had an older brother, Frank, who passed away in 1998 and a younger brother, Wilfred, who drowned in the Aba River at the age of twelve.

After primary school, he went to a standard (high) school at Enitonia in Port Harcourt. Dad was one of the three people in the whole community that went to a standard school in his time. Due to the nature of his father's business as a transporter of goods, he spent some of his younger years in Northern part of Nigeria, then in Southern Nigeria; in Port Harcourt before settling in Aba. Dad was a prolific soccer player hence he played professionally for the cities in the North, in Port Harcourt and in Aba.

Dad met his wife, Gladys Belugbo, in 1948 when she came to Aba from Port Harcourt to visit a relative who happened to be living in his father's property. He vowed he must surely marry her and he did. When the time came to pay her dowry, his father kept his diesel truck running through the ceremony to the amazement of the villagers who had not seen anything like that before. My father and grandfather were show promoters. Dad and mom multiplied and became very fruitful and were blessed with five boys and four girls, twenty eight grandchildren, and great grandchildren.

Church of Christ of Latter Day Saints (LDS)

Dad's quest for the knowledge of our Lord and savior, Jesus Christ, led the family to LDS. According to E. Dale LeBaron in August 1990 *Gospel Pioneers in Africa*, he writes: "Although the Church was established in South Africa in 1853, more than a century passed before work officially began among blacks in Africa. In 1960, Glen G. Fisher returned from South Africa after serving as mission president there. The First Presidency asked him to stop in Nigeria and investigate groups which had organized themselves into church units and had taken the name of The Church of Jesus Christ of Latter-day Saints. For the next six years, Church leaders made efforts to send missionaries to Nigeria. In fact, President David O. McKay set apart Brother LaMar Williams for this work. Others were also called, but the effort was abandoned in 1966 when visas could not be obtained."

Having brought LDS to Nigeria with an associate, Mr. Agu, dad became the leader when his friend left the church. He opened a paint business with the help of the church. We worshipped in our house which was the headquarters. We had mounted a large LDS sign on the mango tree in the front of our house.

Dad had many roles in the church including overseer and leader of the church in Nigeria He was very instrumental in bringing an outreach program to the Cross River area, also in Southern Nigeria

Dad fought in the courts to have the church legalized and to be recognized amidst insults because of discrimination as blacks could not become priests. There were many people who were not pleased with the church policy. That, perhaps, explained why visas were not obtainable in 1966. There was also much instability in Nigeria which resulted in a civil war.

Dad shielded the church from embarrassment and protected its interest.

At one point, Mr. Lamar Williams on one of his trips to Aba was going to be arrested to humiliate the church and Dad had to put a stop to it.

When Elder Tanner, came to Aba, a special song was composed for him; he was impressed on how well Dad understood the teachings of Joseph Smith and was able to teach others. The picture on the right shows two young women, on mission work from Canada, perhaps that we worshipped with. I believe on the left of the picture is Sister Hansen; I don't remember the name of the other young woman. Picture was taken prior to the civil war around 1966 or 1967 by Countryman Studio in Aba.

Dad led the Church until the outbreak of civil war in 1967 between Biafra and Nigeria. When the war came closer to Aba, we moved and lost contact with Utah and things were never the same. Shortly thereafter in 1968 or so, we lost our youngest brother, John. In 1970, we lost Christiana as well at the age of 5. It was a devastating loss. She was the apple of Dad's eyes.

I am reminded of the song, I don't know about tomorrow for its skies may turn to gray, but Jesus knows what lies ahead. With shadow of death hovering over us, the skies were really gray, but Jesus indeed knows what lies ahead.

Shortly after the civil war, people were broke and some unscrupulous folks came to Dad and urged him to bring the "white" people back. Dad suspected they had other things in their minds and in their hearts. Dad simply told them to write Utah themselves if they so desired.

I used think in my younger years that if LDS had moved the family out of harm's way, out of Biafra into Cameroun or any of the neighboring peaceful countries, or even brought us to America or Canada like some other religious groups did to their key members that the family might still be members of the church with controlling authority in Nigeria and that we wouldn't have lost John and Christiana. I felt like they blew it, that they didn't care that much for their point man in Nigeria. They were not there for us when we needed them the most.

Then I was reminded of Jeremiah 29:11 with an assuring word and that settled me down. It says, son, "I know the thoughts I think towards you, thoughts of peace, and not of evil, to give you and your family an expected end"

LDS attempted though to have us back to the church. In the article titled, President Hinckey Dedicates the Aba, Nigeria Temple, by Julie Dockstader Heaps, deseretnews.com; she writes "The history of the LDS Church in Nigeria goes back as far as the 1950s, when some Nigerians learned about the church through magazine articles. After acquiring some literature, groups of people began meeting unofficially in the church's name. After the 1978 revelation that extended the priesthood to every faithful, worthy man in the church the first missionaries were sent back to Nigeria and Ghana.

So, in 1978 following the revelation, LDS delegates came to our house in Aba for a visit. They came to make their final pitch for the family to return to the church and to resume the leadership role. We were also made aware of a possible LDS Temple to be built in Aba. In return Dad would become, perhaps, the first black priest in Nigeria, his children would be brought to America. If these offers had been made prior to the civil war in 1967 or earlier, things might have been different. At the time, there could not have been in my opinion any man, black or white out of Africa more deserving of priesthood than Dad. It appeared LDS would have to continue their journey in Nigeria without the family. This is how the only LDS Temple in all of Nigeria came to be built in Aba.

Upon the death of my grandfather, Chief Israel Oparaiwu Onwuelezi in 1986, the communities came to Dad to continue after his father, but he declined. His father was a ruler in some certain Mbieri communities for over fifty years. The title was then conferred unto Eze Henry Madumere, of the same kindred as my paternal grandmother and whose son is now the Deputy Governor of Imo State.

I would like to dedicate this song by Rhea F. Miller to my Dad:

I'd rather have Jesus than silver or gold;

I'd rather be His than have riches untold;

I'd rather have Jesus than houses or lands;

I'd rather be led by His nail-pierced hand

Refrain:

Than to be the king of a vast domain

And be held in sin's dread sway;

I'd rather have Jesus than anything

This world affords today.

Assembly of God Church, Nigeria

As a member of the Assembly of God Church, dad and mom purchased lands and built the first Assembly of God church and the parsonage in our village community as well as in my maternal village less the parsonage. I learned from my dad, that it is always better to give than to receive. Dad was a compassionate fellow, a humanitarian, a professional soccer player, a chorister, an excellent accordionist, a church builder, a loving father to his children, a husband for almost sixty five years and a believer in the saving grace of our Lord and savior, Jesus Christ.

Dad was a humble and a quiet man who when the things of this world were laid down at his feet, they did not move him. As Apostle Paul stated in Philippians Chapter 3:8, "More than that, I count all things to be loss in view of the surpassing value of knowing Christ Jesus my Lord, for whom I have suffered the loss of all things, and count them but rubbish so that I may gain Christ".

His journey here on Earth ended on June 29th, 2012. It was calm and peaceful. He was preceded in death by son, John and daughter, Christiana, his parents, and two brothers. His was a life well lived, to God be the glory.

To God be the glory, great things He has done;

So loved He the world that He gave us His Son,

Who yielded His life atonement for sin,

And opened the life gate that all may go in.

Refrain:

Praise the Lord, praise the Lord,

Let the earth hear His voice!

Praise the Lord, praise the Lord,

Let the people rejoice!

O come to the Father, through Jesus the Son,

And give Him the glory, great things He has done.

O perfect redemption, the purchase of blood,

To every believer the promise of God;

The vilest offender who truly believes,

That moment from Jesus a pardon receives.

Refrain:

Praise the Lord, praise the Lord,

Let the earth hear His voice!

Praise the Lord, praise the Lord,

Let the people rejoice!

O come to the Father, through Jesus the Son,

And give Him the glory, great things He has done.

Great things He has taught us, great things He has done,

And great our rejoicing through Jesus the Son;

But purer, and higher, and greater will be

Our wonder, our transport, when Jesus we see.

Refrain:

Praise the Lord, praise the Lord,

Let the earth hear His voice!

Praise the Lord, praise the Lord,

Let the people rejoice!

COMMENTARY ON 2012 USA PRESIDENTIAL ELECTION

What lesson, one might asked, is learned from the last presidential election in the United States of America between President Barak Obama and Governor Mitt Romney. I am sure, it is many and varied depending on one's race, political affiliation or ideology or religion.

It was an election where some voters felt they could not vote for Romney because of his affiliation with the church of Mormon. Those people among other things voted for President Obama because they believed he will protect their economic interests though a substantial number of them, Blacks and Hispanics opposed or appeared to oppose his position on same sex marriage because it is very detrimental to their already fragmented family structure and against their beliefs as stipulated in the Bible or judging from defeated referendums of these issues in many states.

President Obama won the election to the shock and amazement of naysayers who were sure he would be defeated because of these and other issues, notably for his party affiliation not wanting anything to do with or mention of the name, God, in their political platform until persuaded to so or President Obama desiring that the state of Israel pull back to pre-1967 "indefensible" boarder with Palestine, that in essence calls for the partition of Jerusalem into East and West. The issue becomes why Christians and Jews would vote for someone or a political party that appeared, in words and actions, to stand contrary to their beliefs and interests such as calling for partition of Jerusalem.

It has been asked of Christians, what does Jerusalem; the city of David, mean to them, what the Bible says about this city, and about the return of Christ? It is of some people's opinion that this was a critical issue church leaders and congregations, mostly of blacks and Hispanics did not or chose not to understand or care about because of ignorance or false indoctrination. They see this as mind boggling and incomprehensible to say the least as people of other faith such as the Moslems understand this issue well and they vote accordingly.

They are also of the opinion that some issues are bigger than amnesty, food stamps, government subsidies and handouts, look, race, manner of speech and personalities of political aspirants.

Some of President Obama's distracters and political opponents see him as an "Affirmative" President who was elected the first time not because of his political leadership, experience, or management because he had none, but because he is black. They did not think he deserved another four years of unproductive or sub-par presidency both at home as well as in international relations.

They believe that a litany of recent as well as past events have proven them right. They are of the opinion that, our enemies do not fear us and our friends do not trust us. They cited the mishandling and the deception of Benghazi's, Libya, affairs following the death of our ambassador and three other men. Their deaths were deliberately blamed on mere riots instead of attributing them to an organized attack by a heavily armed group.

The NSA's domestic and allied countries Surveillance's program; the debacle of Affordable Care Act, fondly known as Obama Care have given President Obama's political opponents even more ammunition to attack him as being inexperience, untruthful, and untrustworthy.

Even the most recent agreement with Iran over her nuclear program has become a concern for many within the United States, Israel, Saudi Arabia, Turkey, etc. They look at it as an exercise in futility which will eventually go the way of North Korea. Your guess is just as good as mine what the State of Israel might do next. Here is a part of speech given by Israeli Prime Minister, Benjamin Netanyahu at the United Nations General Assembly on October 1, 2013.

"Yet Iran faces one big problem, and that problem can be summed up in one word: sanctions. I have argued for many years, including on this podium, that the only way to peacefully prevent Iran from developing nuclear weapons is to combine tough sanctions with a credible military threat. And that policy today is bearing fruit. Thanks to the efforts of many countries, many represented here, and under the leadership of the United States, tough sanctions have taken a big bite off the Iranian economy".

The agreement in Geneva on Sunday, November 24, 2013 called for lifting of sanctions against Iran which most observers believed were working well to deter Iran's effort in her bid for a nuclear arsenal. But why would the POTUS, Obama and his administration thought this is the right policy to pursue at this time over the objection of the state of Israel and others? These observers now believe that with lifting of sanctions, Iran is on track to developing nuclear weapon capability sooner than later. We are now undoubtedly on a collision course in the Middle East all things being equal.

"Ladies and gentlemen, Israel will never acquiesce to nuclear arms in the hands of a rogue regime that repeatedly promises to wipe us off the map. Against such a threat, Israel will have no choice but to defend itself.

I want there to be no confusion on this point. Israel will not allow Iran to get nuclear weapons. If Israel is forced to stand alone, Israel will stand alone. Yet, in standing alone, Israel will know that we will be defending many, many others".

I am sure President Obama's supporters did not and would not even now subscribe to these sentiments. They believed he brought the nation back from collapse following economic meltdown at the tail end of President George W. Bush presidency as one financial institution after another failed or at the brink of failure. A chief proponent of same sex marriage, abortion rights and a darling of the progressives and the media who thinks the opposition party, the Republicans, are impediments to his agenda of transformation of America into a more secular society.

It was a very divisive elections; many rejoicing on the outcome whereas the hearts of many failed. And so it was in the year 2012, month 11, day 6 as one puts it, that the people of United States of America wanted to be like other nations, like the Europeans, like children of Israel were. Having lost their moral bearing and confidence in Him who had guided them all along, God granted their request. Obama, Obama, Obama, they chanted, yes we can! Some are of the opinion that this election marked a turning point for the people of the United States of America.

They became or were on their way to be like other nations and moved or started moving away from their confession of faith, IN GOD WE TRUST over economic reasons and over their eight foot king, "Saul". They did not think that Pat Robertson was wrong predicting Obama's defeat, or Billy Graham endorsing Romney, or John Hagee urging believers to vote the Bible were wrong or Gov. Mitt Romney paying 15% or whatever tax on capital gains as stipulated in the tax code. It was they believed God granted the wishes of Americans desiring to be like other nations.

What will it all mean?

1 Timothy 4:1 tells us that, The Spirit clearly says that in later times some will abandon the faith (apostasy, falling away or defection from faith) and follow deceiving spirits and things taught by demons. "In our word apostasy; and by this term we understand a dereliction of the essential principles of religious truth - either a total abandonment of

Christianity itself, or such a corruption of its doctrines as renders the whole system completely inefficient to salvation", Clarke's commentary.

From Pope Francis: "It is not necessary to talk about these issues (abortion, gay marriage and contraception) all the time. The dogmatic and moral teachings of the church are not all equivalent. The church's pastoral ministry cannot be obsessed with the transmission of a disjointed multitude of doctrines to be imposed insistently.

"We have to find a new balance," the pope continued, "otherwise even the moral edifice of the church is likely to fall like a house of cards, losing the freshness and fragrance of the Gospel." he criticized the church for putting dogma before love, and for prioritizing moral doctrines over serving the poor and marginalized. He articulated his vision of an inclusive church, a "home for all"

"An inclusive church, a home for all" What exactly do these phrases mean? Does it mean a comprising church or social engineering in the church?

The Bible clearly stated that, no man might buy or sell, except he that had the mark, or the name of the beast, or the number of his name. Rev 13:17.

It is the opinion of some people that the mark of the Beast would not be forced upon anyone because they believe that majority of Americans would resist vigorously. The mark rather would be accepted willingly by virtue of the Beast policies that would lead to loss of economic freedom thereby fostering dependency on the government for monetary handouts and for sustenance or enhancing one economic survival such as granting legal statues to illegal aliens that they may work, buy, and trade. And as such one cannot bit the fingers that feed him or he will starve. After all "He who pays the piper calls the tune". Consequently, you turn blind eyes to the piper or to him whose fingers feed you as he leads you deeper into the path of unrighteousness and away from God's precepts. Apostasy makes this possible.

With the loss of economic independency and legislations trying to outlaw right to bear certain arms, Americans would be sitting ducks for the man of the hour to want to bring America to its knees. They believe this is predicated on the fact that America would be weaken at home and at abroad by her insurmountable debts, and welfare statehood and that would handicapped United States of America from continuing to be a dominant power in the world as we know it now. Eventually, America would go the way of what was once a powerful nation, Great Britain.

Consider John 14:1, "Let not your heart be troubled; you believe in God, believe also in me". It is my belief that God's divine plans and purposes are being worked out for our lives even now. The author is not suggesting in any form or fashion that President Obama is the Beast or anything like that but rather writing about possible ways "Mark of the Beast" would be obtain when he the "Son of Perdition" eventually arrives at the stage to take his place.

ABOUT THE AUTHOR

Ben-el Onwuelezi is an aspiring author who has previously written three children books: *Ants Everywhere*, *Revolution in the Colony of Ants*, and the *Daddy's Princess*. His latest book, *In His Time*, is from the heart as he looks at some of the issues facing the body of Christ, the Church today. One of the biggest issue as he sees it is, falling away or apostasy. With that comes moral relativism, obliteration, alteration, or watering down of once firmly held Biblical beliefs and non-adherence to God's precepts and commandments.

He is also the founder and president of Sub Saharan Turning Point (SSTP), a non- governmental organization. SSTP is established to help rebuild "Walls" of Sub Saharan communities. Tax exempt status application is pending with Internal Revenue Service.

Ben-el Onwuelezi is a registered pharmacist by profession. He and his family lives in Rowlett, Rockwall County in the great state of Texas.

Other books in the pipeline

Redemption in the Midst of Chaos - An Autobiography The book takes you through my early childhood, our struggle for survival during the civil war in Nigeria. Here is an excerpt from the book after we left Aba to the village side at the height of the conflict.

Because my parents didn't know all the less traveled interior pathways into the hinterlands or to other remote villages, we found ourselves heading to a place called Orji where there was heavy fighting. We kept moving to different places, wherever we felt secured with whatever essential belongings we can afford to carry. We were now refugees in every sense of the word. Our movement was made more difficult because we were young children, from one to eight years old, who can only walk but short distances at a time. These are any parent's nightmare, how to get the young tired legs from one destination to the other.

Now that I am a lot older, I cannot help but wonder if one can draw an analogy with the great tribulation mentioned in Matthew Chapter 24:19. It says, "But woe to those who are pregnant and to those who are nursing babies in those days". One can easily read this passage to mean, woe to those who are with children and toddlers. In verse 22 & 23, it says in paraphrasing that no one can survive the tribulation if those days were not shortened, but the days nevertheless will be shortened only for the sake of the elect.

Moving from place to place in search of food and shelter eventually caught up with us. We couldn't walk; we were tired, hungry, dirty, and miserable. My brother, who is about eighteen months older, always talked about in jest how he carried me on his back and trekked for long distances. It wasn't long before we started developing symptoms of malnutrition, kwashiorkor it was called: protruded stomach, sunken eyeballs, hair changing color, and pale skin. Food was very scarce; we needed proteins and edible green leaves badly. We experimented with leaves we hadn't eating before and got our proteins from eating fried lizards. Let me tell you, "them" marinated lizard meats taste better than jerky beef.

These were tough, hard, and perilous times for my parents and my older siblings, who were young teenagers at this time. I remembered quite well John, the youngest, crying a lot as he was supposedly in distress tugging on my mother's garment as most toddlers do. He would shortly thereafter succumb to malnutrition and disease I supposed. Having lost the youngest one, the rest of us were still not out of the wood yet for we were in desperate need for food, powdered milk and medications. The issue becomes as far as my parents were concerned was not to dwell too much on the dead child, but on the ones living who are going to meet the same faith as their little brother if nothing gets done quickly. Woe indeed to those with young children!

You will read in the book how we came to accept Jesus Christ through a little girl we met at a train station. Here we were hungry, thirsty, and miserable. The little girl's family did give us water and something much more than that. They gave us the gospel. They read to us from the gospel of John Chapter 4:13-14 that has remained etched to my soul to this very day: "Whoever drinks of this water will thirst again, but whoever drinks of the water that I shall give him will never thirst. But the water that I shall give will become in him a Fountain of water springing up into everlasting life".

Coming to America: The Story of a Very Savvy Boy from the Bush Country

Here is an excerpt:

The boy's father died climbing a palm tree to tap palm wine. He got distracted by migratory bees, lost his grip and fell to his death. He could climb any tree like a monkey would, never believed in using a harness for support. His death came as a surprise to all who knew him and it became talk of the village and anywhere the news is told. To them, it is like been told that a fish drowned in a river or a monkey falling off a tree. It was even talked about that the gods killed him for some kind of reason. His mother on the other hand, went to a local market to buy and trade food stuffs. On her way back, she got struck by a car. She died from the complication of the accident. This was two years after her husband died. What a sad story!

OTHER PUBLISHED BOOKS
BY THE AUTHOR

Ants Everywhere

This book's objective is to bring into young sub-conscious minds the concept of hard work and diligence. Ezinne by chance met an ant named Anton. Anton, who is a soldier in Queen Antoinette's army is fully equipped and always on the go along with hundreds of other soldier. Anton's invasion of the queen's army into Ezinne's house makes Ezinne realize that Anton is more than just a tiny ant. Ezinne learns a valuable lesson for Anton

Revolution in a Colony of Ants

This book is about dwindling population in a colony of ants and a queen who wants to put a stop to it. Her action deepens the suspicion between her and some members of her colony led by Anton, an army general. This result in unrest as the perpetrators tried to usurp power. Queen Antoinette and her counsel of lower queens were all seized. Anton was banished from the colony as a result of the compromised reached between the combatants.

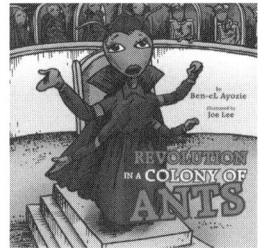

A Daddy's Princess

A dialogue in the book between the princess and her Dad: "Tell me then, why do think you need to make up?" "Dad, the same reason Mom uses makeup." "And what would that be?" "Oh my world, Dad, she is a girl and I'm a girl too." "But she is a big girl and maybe she wants to impress me." "Well Dad, I'm one of your princesses, maybe I want to impress you as well."

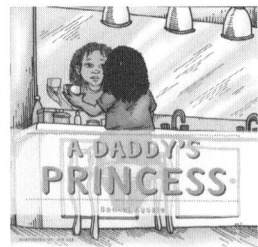

BOOK LAUNCHING

I wish to finish the books in the pipeline and others too. Unfortunately, my work as a pharmacist doesn't give me the much needed time. I would like to take time off work to complete these projects. It would be possible if you would support my books launching drive.

If you would like to support this effort, please visit: www.newvente.com or email me at info@newvente.com